BEARS DON'T CARE

ABOUT YOUR PROBLEMS

BEARS DON'T CARE

ABOUT YOUR PROBLEMS

MORE FUNNY SHIT IN THE WOODS
FROM SEMI-RAD.COM

BRENDAN LEONARD

MOUNTAINEERS
BOOKS

MOUNTAINEERS BOOKS is the publishing division of The Mountaineers, an organization founded in 1906 and dedicated to the exploration, preservation, and enjoyment of outdoor and wilderness areas.

1001 SW Klickitat Way, Suite 201 • Seattle, WA 98134
800.553.4453 • www.mountaineersbooks.org

Printed in China
Distributed in the United Kingdom by Cordee, www.cordee.co.uk

25 24 23 22   2 3 4 5 6

Copyeditor: Erin Moore
Design and layout: Heidi Smets
All illustrations by the author
Cover art by the author

These essays and many of the accompanying illustrations originally appeared on Semi-Rad.com. A version of the story *The Greatest Mountaineering Survival Story Never Told* appeared in the *Mountain Gazette* in 2009.

Library of Congress Cataloging-in-Publication data is on file for this title at https://lccn.loc.gov/2018056006.

Mountaineers Books titles may be purchased for corporate, educational, or other promotional sales, and our authors are available for a wide range of events. For information on special discounts or booking an author, contact our customer service at 800-553-4453 or mbooks@mountaineersbooks.org.

Printed on FSC®-certified materials

MIX
Paper from responsible sources
FSC
www.fsc.org   FSC® C008047

ISBN (paperback): 978-1-68051-270-0
ISBN (ebook): 978-1-68051-271-7

An independent nonprofit publisher since 1960

CONTENTS

FOREWORD

One fine spring night in Utah's San Rafael Swell, about twelve hours before the wind came up and howled ceaselessly for days, I piloted my truck through a crosshatched maze of dirt roads, looking for the one that would bring me, with luck, to the campsite of Brendan Leonard. It was the farthest camp on the farthest track, hidden in the sage and juniper, out of reach of map or GPS, and I was searching for it through bleary eyes after fourteen hours of driving. Well after midnight, my headlights glinted hopefully on the bumper of a vehicle, a tent crouched in the shadows behind. I unwound my stiff limbs, climbed out of my rig, and peered through the windshield of this parked and dusty SUV. There, perched on the dash, was an extra large pizza box with greasy fingerprints all over it, its lid askew. *Yes.* I'd found him.

In 2010 or thereabouts, I was just beginning to put the pieces in place to build *Adventure Journal* from a personal blog to a commercial publishing house, and my life was very much that of a digital hunter and gatherer. I spent my days online searching for story ideas and voices that could convey the uniqueness of the outdoor adventure culture in creative and credible ways. Despite it being the boom years of blogging, though, there wasn't much to hunt or gather, just a whole lot of people saying a whole lot of not much. But then I stumbled upon Semi-Rad.

Everything I was doing that day came screeching to a halt like the Road Runner digging in its heels at the edge of cliff. *Wait, what? Semi-what? Who* was *this guy?* The words were wry, the narrative paths were unexpected, the lessons heartfelt. *Holy smokes,* I thought, *this dude can write*—only I didn't say smokes. By the end of the day, I'd found a mutual friend, got an introduction, and talked Brendan into lending his talents to AJ.

Every generation of outdoor folk has its leading voice. In the 1970s, it was Colin Fletcher, father of the backpacking revolution. In the 1980s, there was Tim Cahill, off having adventures in which he barely survived due to mishap (wild exaggeration being part of the fun). In the 1990s, we had Mark Jenkins, who wrote a column called *The Hard Way* and who, the first time I hiked with him, stuck his leg into a frigid Iceland creek so he could compare the performance of each of his boots. Today, in this post-millennial, rapidly changing, pre-who-knows-what era, there is Brendan Leonard—self-deprecating, open-hearted, considerate, and respectful, the voice of humility and optimism and stoke. No writer I know—and I know a lot of them—better conveys the pleasures and pains, the risks and rewards, and, perhaps most of all, the wonderful absurdities of the outdoor culture.

In these pages, you will find stories about bears, and poop, and love, and inspiration, and you will meet a guide and companion worthy of any adventure, anywhere. If your idea of perfection is a breakfast of cold pizza and hot coffee shared with a friend on the edge of a canyon after a long night of driving, it's exactly the book for you.

—Steve Casimiro
March 2019

INTRODUCTION

One Thursday in February 2011, I clicked "Publish" on a blog post on my new website, Semi-Rad.com. I shared it with my few hundred friends and followers on Twitter and Facebook, and by the end of the day, my website had a few dozen page views. The next week, I wrote and published a new post, and the next week I published another one. I told myself I'd keep writing one blog post per week until something happened, or I got sick of it. I had paid $15 for the URL, and used free WordPress software and an inexpensive theme to create the blog, so all it was really costing me was my time.

I wanted to be an adventure writer, and had been trying to get a foothold in all the major outdoor magazines since 2004, but hadn't had much luck. I had a lot of things I wanted to say about what I felt and observed while climbing, backpacking, trail running, and skiing in the Colorado mountains and the desert, but a lot of it was too goofy or out there to pitch to magazine editors. So I started publishing it on my own.

A few months in, I published a semi-facetious guide to how much beer you should buy a friend in exchange for favors related to the outdoors, like borrowing a pair of skis or having someone dig you out of an avalanche. It took off a bit, and a few hundred people visited my website—including Steve Casimiro from *Adventure Journal*. Steve was the first outdoor media professional to notice, believe in, and then amplify anything about Semi-Rad.com. He republished some of my work, vaulting it into a much bigger arena.

Within a few months, I had written a couple dozen posts, one every week, just like I promised myself—and something was happening. I kept at it, writing what I thought was my best work every week, and gradually other opportunities popped up. I started to get more writing assignments, became a contributing editor at *Adventure Journal*, then *Climbing* magazine, and had just enough work coming in to take the leap into full-time freelance writing. One day in August 2012, I sent my work laptop back to my tech company employer, cringing as I slid it across the counter at the shipping office, ending my brief tenure as a well-paid remote copywriter with cushy benefits.

The gamble paid off, and I've made a career of telling adventure stories. Over the years, my writing started to make its way into all those magazines I dreamed about working for, the ones I thought would never publish my stuff: *Climbing, Outside, Backpacker, Alpinist, Adventure Cyclist, High Country News*. But every week, my first priority was to put my best idea on Semi-Rad.com, because I thought and hoped a few hundred people were counting on it every Thursday morning.

In November 2015, my friend Jim Harris sent me a message from a hostel in southern Chile. He had been sitting around a fireplace with a few other people he didn't know when they started to crack some jokes about the fire, referencing something called "Obsessive Campfire Adjustment Syndrome." Jim asked, "Are you guys talking about that Semi-Rad blog post?" And they said yes, they were.

"Do You Have Obsessive Campfire Adjustment Syndrome?" didn't break the internet. It did well and reached a few hundred or a few thousand people, as far as I could tell. It didn't come close to being the most widely-read blog post on Semi-Rad.com, yet people halfway around the world somehow were laughing at it, months later, in front of a fireplace. I don't remember having exact goals for my website, but creating a piece of writing that becomes a joke between friends, that lives on in conversation and brings a little bit of joy or fun between complete strangers, is one of the best outcomes possible.

When I started Semi-Rad.com, I just wanted to write about the outdoors. I had some ideas that I thought other people might want to read, and that would make them laugh—hoping they might see some of their own experiences in the things I wrote. I always wanted to write, not about myself or about "them," the people you make fun of sometimes—but about "us," outdoorsfolk. And we're a curious lot. We like to sleep on the ground, stay outside in bad weather, push ourselves physically to the point of near-exhaustion, and in general do a lot of things most of the civilized world thinks are ridiculous. But there's also meaning in what we do, and humor, and I am grateful that I've been able to spend hundreds of hours since 2011 staring at my keyboard trying to tell those stories and put those things down in a few hundred words every week.

This book collects seventy-nine of the most read, most shared, most commented-on pieces that have been published on Semi-Rad.com since it began. I hope they make you laugh, or make you think, or inspire you to call a friend to go do something outside with you.

MAKE THIS YEAR THE YEAR OF MAXIMUM ENTHUSIASM

One Saturday morning last October, my friend Greg and I were running down the North Kaibab Trail in the Grand Canyon, close to halfway through 26 miles of trail. We had run 4 miles and would run about 4 more to Phantom Ranch, where we could double-fist coffee and Lemmy lemonade at the cantina before climbing 4,400 vertical feet back up the South Rim to finish a hike/run Rim-to-Rim.

I turned around mid-stride and said, "Hey, Greg!"

"Yeah," he said.

"We're running in the Grand Canyon!"

Sometimes I get to do awesome things, and I kind of forget how awesome they are. Do you? I get stressed, caught up in other stuff, and I forget how fortunate I am, how incredible life has turned out to be most days, and some of the special places I've gotten to see. Most of the time, though, I try to keep a pretty good handle on it—I remember to turn around and yell to my friend that, yes, we are running across the most famous hole on Earth, and that's pretty special. Or, you know, even reminding someone a few months later about something special:

Brendan <brendan@semi-rad.com>   Sun, Dec 15, 9:15 PM ☆ ↰ :
to Tom ▾

Remember when we climbed Cathedral Peak? That shit was SICK!

Tom <Tom@▬▬▬.com>   Mon, Dec 16, 8:05AM ☆ ↰ :
to me ▾

I just got into work and this is the first email I read. I laughed out loud and I'm smiling like an idiot. Probably will be all day. That shit was SICK!

Kurt Vonnegut, in a 2003 speech to students at the University of Wisconsin, said, "I urge you to please notice when you are happy, and exclaim or murmur or think at some point, 'If this isn't nice, I don't know what is.'"

This year, I urge you to notice when something is awesome, as it often is, and exclaim or murmur or just make a mental note of it. Isn't it just goddamn fantastic that you have your health, for example? Or running water, or electricity? Or that you have enough money to actually pay someone else to make you a cup of coffee? Or if you want ice cream, you are at any time in America probably only five or ten minutes away from a place that sells some form of it? (Trust me on that one.)

Your life, even the bad parts, is fucking amazing. And most of the small things that make up your life are amazing, too—mountain bike rides, rock climbs, ski runs, sunsets, stars, friends, people, girlfriends and boyfriends, dogs, songs, movies, jokes, smiles . . . hell, even that burrito you ate for lunch today was pretty phenomenal, wasn't it?

What was your enthusiasm for these things last year? I recommend you step it up this year.

People can disagree on things like quality, their friend's taste in food, or whether or not a movie is good. But no one can argue with enthusiasm, especially when it is over the top.

Do you think that climb you just did is the greatest climb ever? Great! If someone tries to tell you it isn't, who cares? Greatest Rock Climb Ever is not an objective title. Thusly, when you are excited about a climb—or a trail run or a summit view or a bike ride or a sunrise— don't let anyone bring you down.

A conversation where someone puts down your favorite ski area/ mountain/rock climb/trail/burrito is not a conversation about ski areas/mountains/rock climbs/trails/burritos. It is a conversation about that person being a pompous asshole. Go forth and be positive this year.

Enthusiasm doesn't have to stand up to criticism. It doesn't even have to really make sense. If you finish a ski run, MTB trail, or sport climbing route, and you love it, I encourage you to try out new superlatives when describing it to someone else. This goes for everything you're excited about. Examples:

- "I'm just going to tell you now that *Outer Space* is the most incredible rock climb you will ever do. You cannot not smile while climbing it. It's like the Beatles. Even if you for some ridiculous reason don't enjoy it, you can't deny its inherent goodness."
- "Have you heard the new Talib Kweli song? It will knock you on your ass!"
- "The eggplant parmesan sub at Pasquini's is probably my favorite sandwich in the entire city of Denver, if not the state of Colorado. In fact, now that I've said that, I think we should go to Pasquini's immediately."

Maybe some of the stuff you love, that you're passionate about, isn't cool. Hey, this is is a brave new world. Everything is cool. Irony is either everything, or dead. Be honest: When you see someone wearing a Motley Crue T-shirt, you don't know if they're serious or wearing it to be ironic, do you? So, do you like Motley Crue? Then ROCK THAT SHIT. And spread happiness.

Remember, it is not illegal to high-five anyone. Do you use exclamation points in the salutations of your emails? Well, why not?

Do you like to laugh? Most people do, don't they, including baristas, waitstaff, and retail personnel. Perhaps you have at some point had a real conversation with one of these people. This can sometimes begin by sincerely asking those people how they are, instead of treating them like a machine that makes you coffee or orders your salad. This opens the door to making them laugh. If you play your cards right, you may be able to high-five them at the end of a conversation.

Remember yesterday, when you saw that one thing that reminded you of that one friend of yours, and you thought about how if you sent that friend a photo of the thing that reminded you of them, they would smile? But then you didn't send your friend that photo, and it wasn't awesome. Don't do that again. Here's what you do:

1. Take the photo.
2. Send it to your friend.
3. Your friend smiles. The world is a better place. Thanks.

You may have already made some New Year's resolutions: to lose weight, to eat better, to read two books every month, whatever. How about making one more, to be just a little more awesome?

NINE REASONS WHY YOU SHOULD NEVER BIKE TO WORK

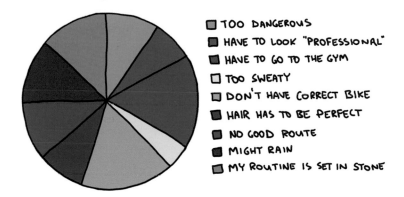

☐ TOO DANGEROUS
☐ HAVE TO LOOK "PROFESSIONAL"
☐ HAVE TO GO TO THE GYM
☐ TOO SWEATY
☐ DON'T HAVE CORRECT BIKE
☐ HAIR HAS TO BE PERFECT
☐ NO GOOD ROUTE
☐ MIGHT RAIN
☐ MY ROUTINE IS SET IN STONE

I have biked everywhere within four miles of my apartment in the past five years, including every job I've had—so, though I live and work in Denver, I've never had to drive to work in Denver. I find riding a bicycle exhilarating, but there's no reason for you to think you should. In fact, here are nine reasons you shouldn't bike to work.

9. IT'S TOO DANGEROUS.

Can you imagine being out there on a bicycle with all these crazy drivers flying past you, nothing to protect you except a plastic and styrofoam shell on your head? You could get killed. The absolute best thing to do is to stay in the protective cage of your car, because of course no one's ever been killed when they're inside an automobile. Driving is safe.

8. YOU HAVE TO WEAR A TIE TO WORK. OR A SUIT. OR A SKIRT.

Not only that, it's important to wear your tie/suit/business casual attire from the moment you leave your house in the morning until the moment you get home. There is no conceivable way you could leave some clothes at your office, and change into them after you ride your bike to work, two or three days a week. Plus, your suit/tie combination is so dialed, you can't just spread your tie collection out over two locations. Where the hell is my cornflower blue tie? I need to see if it looks good with these shoes. And, like, there's some way to ride a bike in a skirt or a dress?

7. YOU HAVE TO GO TO THE GYM AFTER/BEFORE WORK.

What, you're supposed to carry all your work materials and your gym clothes in a tiny little backpack on a bike? Please. I mean, what, bike to work, then bike to the gym, then get on the stationary bike for forty-five minutes, and bike home? Ridiculous. What are you, Lance Armstrong? I guess you could just ride your real bike, and stop going to the gym, but, hey, we're Americans. We work out *indoors*.

6. YOU CAN'T SHOW UP ALL SWEATY AND SMELLY FOR YOUR JOB.

It is a proven fact that once you have sweated from exercise, you can never recover until you get into a shower or bath and rinse it off. Also a fact: Human sweat is comprised of more than 90 percent fecal particles, which is why you smell like a hog confinement instantly after you start exercising, as well as afterward, when the people next to you on the Stairmaster are passing out like they've just been chloroformed. It's not like you could take a shower at the office, after all, or use Action Wipes to wipe off when you get to work to mitigate that smell. Your co-workers will be all, "Bob, what the hell did you do, bike to work today? It smells like somebody's gutting a week-old deer carcass in your cubicle."

5. YOU DON'T HAVE THE RIGHT BIKE FOR IT.

The only bikes you own are your Trek Madone and your single-speed 29er, neither of which will work. You'd have to go out and buy a dedicated commuting bike, which start at, what, $1,200? Ask those day laborer guys who bike to work every day on secondhand Huffys and Magnas—they're not cheap.

4. YOU CAN'T BE WEARING A BIKE HELMET AND MESSING UP YOUR HAIR BEFORE WORK.

Fact: Hair products are not portable, and are not designed for use outside of your home bathroom or a hair salon. And let's face it: Your hairstyle is a work of carefully crafted art, not something that can be rushed in five, ten, or even thirty minutes in some modern office restroom. You spend a long time on your hair, just like Tony Manero. You can't just throw it all away on a bike ride.

3. THE ROUTE FROM YOUR HOME TO YOUR OFFICE WOULD BE SUICIDE ON A BIKE.

There are no bike lanes, no shoulders, no wide sidewalks, no nothing on the roads from your home to your office. What, are you supposed to find other roads to ride on, like lesser-traveled, lower-speed-limit roads through residential areas? Or detour way out of your way to get on a bike path? No thank you. You don't have time for that shit.

2. WHAT IF IT RAINS?

Yeah, Mr. Hardcore Bike Commuter, what if it rains? You're supposed to just ride a bicycle home from the office through a downpour? What are you supposed to do when you get home, looking like a sewer rat? This is a civilized society. Thanks to umbrellas, sprinting from your car to your office, and sometimes holding a newspaper above your head, you haven't gotten wet outside of your shower since 2007. Next thing, someone's going to tell you that you have to carry a rain jacket in your bike commuting bag—maybe pants too. What the hell is this, a backpacking trip? You're just trying to get to work on time.

1. YOU WOULD HAVE TO CHANGE YOUR ROUTINE.

Please. Give up your forty-five-minute drive into work, the drive that energizes you for the day ahead? Give up interacting with all those other fun, friendly, courteous drivers on the freeway? Sitting in traffic? Road construction? Merging? Not a chance.

These are just nine reasons you shouldn't bike to work. I'm sure you can think of others.

HOPEFULLY THIS BEER IS THANKS ENOUGH: A GRATITUDE SCALE FOR OUTDOORSFOLK

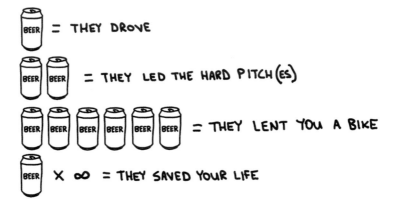

Last Wednesday, I was standing in my neighborhood liquor store trying to decide whether I should buy a bottle of Scotch or a six-pack of good beer for a friend of mine. I was borrowing his set of ice tools, and seven ice screws, for a trip to the Ouray Ice Park. My girlfriend does not own ice tools, and I do not yet own any ice screws. And I am big on appreciation. I figure we're talking $400 worth of screws, and $400 worth of ice tools, so he's saving me quite a bit of money by allowing me to postpone my investment.

Hmm, $11 worth of Dale's Pale Ale ought to cover it. I decided a bottle of Scotch would be way over the top.

I was thinking, though, for a guy who doesn't drink, I seem to purchase my fair share of beer, in liquor stores and at bars. Maybe it's because, in my hometown in Iowa, beer is currency. I bought my first car for $500 and two cases of Busch Light. My father once rented a skid-loader for a day in exchange for eight steaks and four cases of beer. My friend's father once picked up a topper for his pickup truck for $15 and a handle of Black Velvet.

There are certain unspoken levels of appropriate gratitude—you wouldn't ask your friend to help you move furniture all day and buy him/her one drink. No, you would buy them pizza and a bunch of beer, at minimum. It's the same for the outdoors. I've come up with some rough guidelines to help you decide what's appropriate when thanking someone for an outdoor-related favor.

ONE BEER:

- Friend/climbing partner picked you up and drove to the trailhead.
- You forgot to pack a tire patch kit or extra tube, you got a flat tire, your friend let you borrow their tube/patch.
- You borrowed a guidebook.
- You ran out of water on a hike and your friend split their last bottle of water with you.
- You were very late getting home from hiking/climbing; friend/climbing partner allowed you to tell your spouse that it was his/her fault you were late.

TWO BEERS:

- Friend/climbing partner picked you up and drove to the trailhead while you slept in the passenger seat.
- Friend/climbing partner picked you up and had donuts and/or coffee for you; you did not sleep in the passenger seat on the way to the trailhead.
- Climbing partner led the hard pitch, or pitches.
- You borrowed a pair of skis or snowboard.
- You were very late getting home from hiking/climbing; friend/climbing partner called your spouse and explained that it was his/her fault you were late.
- Friend/climbing partner cooked dinner on overnight trip; it was better than you can cook at home.
- Friend brought firewood for weekend car camping trip.
- You bailed off climbing route, leaving friend's gear (could be more, depending on amount of gear left).

A SIX-PACK:

- You borrowed a set of ice tools and a rack of ice screws.
- You borrowed a sleeping bag, tent, or stove for the weekend.
- Following a bicycle mechanical failure on a road ride way outside of town, your friend drove and picked up you and your bike and took you home.
- You borrowed a friend's mountain bike or road bike.

ONE BEER EVERY TIME YOU GET TOGETHER FOR THE REST OF YOUR LIVES:

- Partner dug you out of an avalanche, full burial.
- Friend ran to get help when you sustained a leg injury in the backcountry and couldn't walk; you survived.

REVIEW: MY RUNNING SHOES

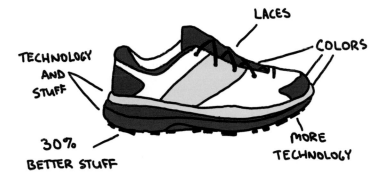

I picked up these sweet-ass rigs after I finally wore out my last pair of trail running shoes after two and a half years (the tread was gone and one of the laces finally snapped). As you can see, there's all sorts of technology and shit in them—there's some plastic stuff on the side, and there are different things to run the laces through, and there's a kind of stretchy thing near the top of the laces. Overall, they're pretty sweet.

I read this book called *Born to Run* a few years ago. You may have heard of it. Author Christopher McDougall investigates the idea that humans are built to run long distances. Among his findings, and you may have heard this before, is the idea that we don't need running shoes to be all that fancy. Some people read the book and bought a pair of barefoot running shoes. I read the same book, but took some of the information as a license to just buy old, cheap shoes and fix the way I ran—which could maybe have previously been described as "Clydesdale," but is now more like "gazelle, shuffling in slow motion."

These shoes are a few years old, I believe—I bought them used at Wilderness Exchange in Denver for $40. I believe they are "trail running shoes," although I also wear them hiking, backpacking, on approach hikes to rock climbs, and for anything else that doesn't require mountaineering boots. Sometimes I end up downclimbing snow slopes in them. They're not waterproof, but that's OK, because I don't think they were designed to be.

Late last summer, the outer mesh stuff kind of gradually sprung a leak over the course of a 30-mile backpacking trip in the Wind River Range in Wyoming, which ended up being just fine as there was no real structural damage.

Of course, since there was kind of a big hole in the outside, I thought maybe I'd get a new pair of shoes before my pal Greg and I did a one-day Rim-to-Rim run in the Grand Canyon last October. I didn't make time to go shoe shopping, so instead of new shoes, I just brought a couple feet of duct tape in my pack in case something catastrophic happened to them and the sole ripped off or something. They made it fine, but later part of something in the toe section was peeling away and got kind of annoying, so I ended up cutting it off with scissors.

Based on my research and testing, I believe the ideal use for these shoes is running on trails, or running on other surfaces, and I guess walking too. But also based on my research, you can do basically whatever the hell you want in them. I wore them to hike into a back-country ski run once, have bicycled in them up to about five miles at a time, and I think I played my dad in pool once in them too. I also noted that they performed well when I wore them to eat ice cream cones, including this one time I ate two ice cream cones at once because I thought they were really small for $3.50 each. Essentially, you can count on these shoes.

Or, I guess, you can count on most shoes. I don't really have too many problems with running shoes. I've never been out on a run and said, "Man, I can't go on. These shoes are just not high-quality enough." Usually I get about six or eight miles done, and I'm like, "Man, I'm tired," or "I should call my friend and go smash the break-fast tacos at Watercourse," or "I better get back to my phone so I can type in this pithy and witty Facebook status that is bouncing around in my head right now." It's really not the shoes that present obstacles to my running.

I have run several 10Ks in these shoes—not 10K races where you register and get a number and stuff; I just like to run for about sixty or so minutes when I go out and I figure that's about 6 miles or so, which is roughly 10 kilometers. But, you know, these will "go the distance," so to speak, if the distance is like 6 miles. Like if you want to run the Bolder Boulder or something like that. Actually, now that I think of it, I've run about 10 miles in one stretch, too. So go ahead and max them out. I mean, hell, if they can go 10 miles, I imagine they can go 20 or so. I just get bored running that long unless there's food or coffee in the middle somewhere.

Anyway, you should get a pair. Of shoes. Not necessarily these, although I can't complain so far. I think the company that made them a few years ago still makes them. They're not super-flashy right now, but I noticed if you throw them in the washing machine and get some of the dirt out, they look brighter for a few days.

THE GREATEST MOUNTAINEERING SURVIVAL STORY NEVER TOLD

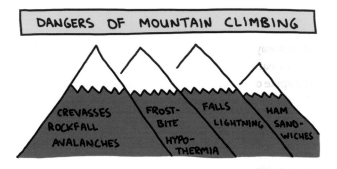

DANGERS OF MOUNTAIN CLIMBING

CREVASSES
ROCKFALL
AVALANCHES

FROST-
BITE
HYPO-
THERMIA

FALLS
LIGHTNING

HAM
SAND-
WICHES

A few years ago, I climbed Drift Peak near Leadville, Colorado, on Presidents' Day with my friend Aaron and my friend Lee. Lee had started up the peak a couple times before in the winter, but bailed for different reasons. He had promised that if we made it to the summit with him on what would be his first successful winter ascent of the peak, he'd tell me the story of how the mountain had "almost killed" him. I expected, of course, another story like the time he was climbing the northwest face of Torreys Peak by himself in the winter and a rock came screaming down the mountain, slamming into his foot and breaking three bones. He had to glissade down 800 feet, then use his ski poles as crutches to hike out the remaining 2.5 miles to his truck, and then drive home to Littleton, where he almost drove through the back wall of his garage because he couldn't get his smashed foot to engage the clutch in time.

The Drift Peak story wasn't quite like that. As we descended the snowy ridge, I was quietly satisfied I had made the summit without throwing up, while Lee had the energy of the Kool-Aid Man. He darted past Aaron and me, yelling, "Gather 'round, Girl Scouts. It's time for a story!"

There he was, his story began, not too far away from where we were sitting, by himself on a cold December day in 2000. He was planning on climbing Fletcher Mountain, a half mile further up past the summit of Drift Peak. He trudged up the snowy ridge, and at the point where the final summit slopes began, he came up on a notch in the ridge. He'd have to climb down a 40-foot slope, then back up a 60-foot slope, to regain the ridge. The second slope was high angle and looked ripe for an avalanche.

Instead, Lee turned around to go home and live to climb another day. The ridge, after all, is colloquially known as "Villa Ridge," named after a man killed by an avalanche on it.

Lee made his way back down the ridge and stopped on top of a large snow dome to eat lunch. It was eleven o'clock in the morning. He jammed the spike of his ice axe into the hard snow and tied his pack to it, anchoring it so it wouldn't slide away. He opened his pack and pulled from it his absolute favorite mountain lunch: A ham-and-cheese sandwich on whole wheat, with mayonnaise and mustard.

This, Girl Scouts, is the "No shit, there I was" part of the story.

Munching on his sandwich, enjoying the view to the south of the Sawatch Range, Lee stopped breathing. He tried to cough, but nothing. His airway was completely blocked by a piece of sandwich. He hacked. Nothing. After ten or so seconds of desperately trying to draw in some thin, 12,900-foot-high air, he began to see a gray frame at the very edge of his vision. He realized he had wasted a lot of time.

He had survived thirty-five years of pushing his limits in the big hills, including hundreds of pitches of roped climbing, that falling rock on Torreys Peak, the occasional incompetent partner, stuck ropes, Rocky Mountain thunderstorms, and more, and he was about to be killed by a goddamn ham sandwich. His story in next year's *Accidents in North American Mountaineering* would be hard to frame as "heroic."

In 1974, American physician Henry J. Heimlich popularized a series of abdominal thrusts that came to be known as "The Heimlich Maneuver," a technique that has saved the lives of many humans who neglect to chew their food completely. The light bulb went on in Lee's oxygen-deprived brain and he remembered the self-Heimlich technique, in which a choking person can Heimlich themselves by leaning over, say, the back of a restaurant chair and pushing it into their diaphragm.

There are no chairs on the northwest ridge of Drift Peak.

But what about wedging the spike of his ice axe against a rock and driving the head of it against his abdomen? Lee looked around. Nothing but snow, which would just give way under his weight. He would have to glissade down the ridge to a talus field 40 feet away to find a large rock: if he could make it in time.

The gray circle around his vision grew larger, and the tunnel of beautiful Colorado mountain scenery shrank. Sixty percent vision now. He frantically fiddled with the knot attaching his ice axe to his pack. Come on, come on, come on. It came free. His pack shot down the slope in front of him. Still, no air.

Lee ripped the ice axe out of the snow and pushed himself into a butt-slide down the slope. He planted the head of his ice axe underneath his ribcage, adze pointing right, pick pointing left. His chest sucked itself into a knot, starving for oxygen.

He picked up speed, lifting his feet in the air so his crampon points didn't catch. His vision tunneled down to 25 percent. At the end of that tunnel was a rock shaped like the state of Tennessee, pointing straight up in the air, flat side facing Lee.

His last thought was, "I'm aiming for Memphis." Just before slamming into the rock, his vision went black. He passed out. Well, he assumes he passed out, because he doesn't remember hitting anything.

He woke up on his back, sucking in air in big gulps, holding a round ball of ham, cheese, mayo, mustard, and whole wheat bread in his mouth. He spat it out.

Everything hurt: stomach, chest, back, shoulders—his hair hurt. The Tennessee-shaped rock sat a foot and a half behind his head. The Rocky Mountain Self-Heimlich had worked. Near as he could tell, the piece of sandwich had dislodged when his ice axe hit rock and the head of the ice axe compressed his diaphragm.

Or, the ham bolus popped out of his throat when he flopped onto his back after doing a full somersault over the rock. While completely unconscious.

Either way, two thoughts popped into his head: "I could have died" and, "but I didn't."

Sitting at the same spot on the ridge eight years later with Aaron and me, Lee closed his story, saying, "And I've never told anybody that story till now, because if my wife had found out, she never would have let me go climbing again."

To which I replied, "Or eat ham sandwiches by yourself." If not for the unfortunate but amicable dissolution of Lee's marriage a few years ago, he may have taken that story to the grave—in his journal for the day, he recorded it simply as "an interesting day."

THE IMPORTANCE OF BEING A LIFELONG BEGINNER

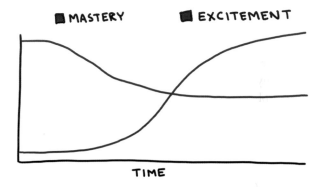

When you dismount a mountain bike going uphill, you end up doing a sort of bow. As you step off and swing a leg over the seat, your head naturally points down as if you are admitting that the trail has you beat—this time.

After years of saying "I suck at fast/gravity/downhill sports," I finally bought a mountain bike a few weeks ago. With this new purchase, I have two goals:

1. I will not crash my new mountain bike hard enough to break anything on my body.
2. I will ride my new mountain bike enough times in the next year that its expensive-to-me-but-apparently-relatively-inexpensive-in-the-world-of-mountain-bikes price feels like an investment and not a foolish endeavor.

I'm a climber, I tell myself. I'm no good at these outdoor sports that require fast reactions: tree skiing, mountain biking, kayaking. I'm in my early thirties, too, which is old enough to know I don't have to do shit I don't want to do, like eat cauliflower, get regular haircuts, wait thirty minutes after eating to get back into the swimming pool, or ride knobby-tired bicycles on steep mountain trails. That's the great thing about being an adult.

Which is also the bad thing about being an adult: thinking you know everything. You know what you can do, and therefore you know what you can't do, too. I'm a bad cook. I can't fix a car. It's too late to go back to college. I don't dance. I'm not a mountain biker.

The last word you'd ever use to describe my friend Elizabeth is "arrogant." Three years ago, I would have introduced her as a boulderer, and a good one. Every year since I met her, she's tried something new: Two years ago, she learned to snowboard. Last winter, she learned to tele ski. This year, she says she's going to learn to roll a kayak. I admire this.

I remember learning to snowboard when I was twenty-six, falling on my ass, and my face, repeatedly, making cartoon-worthy crashes in the middle of blue runs while nine-year-old kids flew by me carving the hell out of everything as I wondered if I'd just given myself a concussion. I was humbled, to say the least. That year, I was able to tell myself, as Elizabeth does every year when she takes up something new: "I am going to try this, I am going to suck at it for an indefinite amount of time, and other people are going to see me fail, repeatedly."

My friend Jeff Weidman started learning to play the guitar at age forty-six, and everyone said he was starting too late in life. He stuck with the lessons and kept practicing, as his career brought big changes almost every other year. Nobody said it was too late in life when he played Bob Dylan's "You Ain't Goin' Nowhere" and John Prine's "Christmas in Prison" at his first-ever open mic six years later.

The earlier you can admit you don't know everything, the more time you have to learn new things and make a richer life. The later you admit you don't know everything, the less time you have. And if you don't admit it at all or ever? There's a song lyric that says, "The older I get, the less I know, and the more I dream."

Is anybody inspired by the guy who knows everything? I'd rather talk to the fat guy at the gym who has finally decided to do something instead of slowly dying in front of his TV, the divorcee going on her first first date in twenty-five years, the shy single guy at the cooking class, all the folks bumbling through our first time in a foreign country and stumbling through a new language, and non-teenagers, like you and me, crashing our new bikes, skis, snowboards, and sheepishly standing up again and believing that these old dogs can learn new tricks.

I'm four for four so far on rides on my new bike without crashing. A couple weeks ago, I swear I caught two inches of air off a small bump in a trail near Fort Collins. If you were standing there and acted quickly, you might have been able to pass a sheet of paper between my tires and the ground.

One friend of mine says we peak as bicycle riders at age thirteen, after which you start to get afraid to jump your bike off things. Another friend says thirty is the new thirteen.

THE IMPORTANCE OF BIG DREAMS

I have a copy of this children's book that I take everywhere I go. It's called *An Awesome Book!*, and everyone I know who's had a baby in the past six months owns a copy, because I bought one for them. It's a kids' book, but I think the message is for adults too.

I like it because it reminds me that I don't need things, but I do need dreams and goals. I need things that I decided I wanted to do one day when I was looking out a window somewhere scratching my chin and thinking about what my life should look like. Also, Dallas Clayton draws incredible unicorns and dinosaurs and bears.

My favorite passage in the book is this:

There are places in the world where people dream up dreams
so simply un-fantastical and practical they seem
to lose all possibility of thinking super things
of dancing wild animals with diamond-coated wings
instead they dream of furniture
of buying a new hat
of owning matching silverware
can you imagine that?

I like to buy books for my friends' children because I think stories are more meaningful than toys, and more memorable. And that goes for adults, too, although sometimes we forget it because we make our lives so hectic.

If you do anything at all in the outdoors, somewhere in your mind is the capacity to dream big and envision yourself doing something amazing. You want to ride the Slickrock Trail, climb El Cap or Mount Rainier, run the NYC Marathon or the Western States 100, or do a raft trip in the Grand Canyon. Maybe you just want to be a climber, or a skier, or a mountain biker. Or marry a beautiful girl, or see the Eiffel Tower, or write a book.

But we get busy. Too busy scrolling our phone screens, watching TV, catching up with all the mundane shit in life and we forget about our dreams. We say things like "I don't have time," and then, when we get frustrated that we don't have enough time, we assuage that feeling of impotence by buying shit we don't need, which we think will make us feel better. Granite countertops, leather sofas—sometimes skis, climbing gear, or bikes we never use. Maybe that's because we're scared of whatever it is we've been thinking about for so long, or maybe it's easier to buy something instead of doing something. Or maybe something we saw told us our dream was something different, and we bought into that.

A few months ago, I was talking to a friend of mine and she told me she had always dreamed of going to Hawaii for her tenth wedding anniversary. I asked, "Are you going?," and she said, "Well, we don't know, for a number of reasons—a new house, some stress and financial things with a new business" . . . et cetera. I said, "I think you gotta put that shit on a credit card if you can and go to Hawaii this year." People go into debt for tens and hundreds of thousands of dollars for the most mundane things—houses, cars, sometimes furniture, sprinkler systems—yet most of us have a hard time sliding our credit card or taking money out of a savings account to pay for what could be the experience of a lifetime.

If you start off a sentence with, "I've always wanted to . . . ", you either

1. aren't going to do it, which means it's not really your dream, or
2. you just haven't done it yet.

Procrastination is fine as long as you're 100 percent sure that you're not going to die in the next year. Because you're going to die someday, and if you're honest with yourself, you will admit that you never once as a kid said to anyone, when I grow up I want matching drapes, or a riding lawn mower that mulches, too, or a cozy living room. You wanted to be a cowboy or a polar explorer or Amelia Earhart.

THE RULES FOR DATING A DIRTBAG

It's a singular feeling when you're thirty-three years old and talking to your mother and she says, "You know what I think you should try? Match.com."

Then there's another feeling when you say to your mother, "Well, Mom, I had this weird feeling about meeting women and telling them I live in a van full of climbing gear, but then I realized I'm really only interested in women who could be interested in a guy who lives in a van full of climbing gear. If that makes any sense." I think my mom is really proud.

There are some interesting things about dating people who love the outdoors, aren't there? Like you fantasize about dating someone who loves to go backpacking, and then you find out that it's really hard to spoon when you're each zipped up in a sleeping bag and it's too cold to put your arms outside of it. And even though you think it would be rad to have a significant other who climbs, you go on a climbing date and are sure your partner/potential girlfriend or boyfriend has lost all respect for you when you get Elvis leg and start whining as you freak out on the crux move a few feet off the belay. Or you want them to live their dreams and you want to live your dreams, but it kind of sucks when they're gone leading a wilderness trip for a month, or you're gone for a two-month bike tour and you have to get out your phone and look at photos of them to remember what they look like.

But then of course, you get all those sunsets and sunrises together, and maybe you get to hold hands during that last wide part of the trail walking to the car, and instead of sitting on a rock somewhere looking over an alpine lake wondering about girls, you get to sit on that same rock with a girl and talk to her about hip hop and books and what she was like in high school and all that.

But is it unromantic to buy your girlfriend an avalanche beacon for Valentine's Day? Because I did that once, and what I thought it said was, "Here's something that means we can spend time together in the backcountry." But I could definitely see someone taking it the wrong way, especially because it came with a shovel.

I mean, I want to open doors for a girl. Give you my jacket when we go to a movie and you're cold walking home. Cook you breakfast when you're sleeping in on a Saturday. But it begins to get fuzzy at the trailhead. Although I'm a gentleman and you're a lady, you will be carrying either the rope, or the rack; the tent, or the stove and fuel and pots. And if I am cooking us dinner over a camp stove, you are setting up the tent, or vice versa. Right?

My friend Teresa went on a couple dates with this guy in Seattle, and she thought it was going pretty well. The third date, she invited him over to barbecue, and they met at a grocery store to pick up a couple things before riding to her house—which, at the time, was at the top of 8th Avenue, a thirty-block, steadily uphill ride into a headwind. He had told her he did some cycling, and had finished a handful of races and road rides. So she was surprised when he stayed behind her for the entire ride up the hill. Into a headwind. The entire ride. "I mean, are you fucking kidding me?" she said when she re-told me the story a couple weeks ago. Either the guy didn't know anything about cycling etiquette and had lied about his experience, or he was a jerk. Either way, that was their last date.

My friend Sara told me last year she was done dating climbers, for a number of reasons. A lot of men she dated seemed to like the *idea* of being with someone who was a climber, but not the reality; or she found herself having more fun climbing with her girlfriends and platonic male friends than climbing with a romantic partner; or the dating pool was just too small if she limited herself only to climbers. Now she's happy with a guy whose main thing is paragliding; he's remembering how to belay and they're climbing together and actually having fun doing it.

Teresa said to me another time, "I just feel like men at the climbing gym are so focused on climbing that they don't notice women." I said, "Are you shitting me? Of course we do. At least I do. As a man, I will tell you there is nothing we are so focused on that we don't notice women. Nothing. We may be too dumb to notice when you are interested, but we never fail to notice women. If I speak for other dudes who are dirtbags, we are especially in tune when we see a woman who exhibits characteristics that suggest she likes to wear backpacks, or sleep in the dirt, or do pull-ups."

Sometimes I say there is no better sound in the world than a beautiful woman laughing, except the sound of a beautiful woman laughing at something I said. But then I think the sound of a beautiful woman yelling, "On belay!" from 120 feet above me is even better. Especially if it comes after she led the crux pitch on the route.

SEVEN TIPS ON HOW TO BE A GOOD TENTMATE

Hey, do you like camping and backpacking with your friends? Of course you do. So obviously you'd like to be invited on lots of trips. How do you get invited on lots of trips? You learn how to be a good tentmate, and to make your tentmate's experience a good one. Here are a few tips on how to do that.

1. **Over-hydrate.** Drink a lot of fluids before you go to bed, to ensure you are well hydrated and able to get up to go pee plenty of times during the night. It is a good idea to put your headlamp in a location where it will be hard to locate when you need to pee, such as the bottom of your sleeping bag. When getting up to pee, maximize movement inside the tent: Don't just unzip your sleeping bag a couple inches and slide out—unzip it all the way down to your ankles. Put on a couple jackets before you go out, maybe even some Gore-Tex. Keep your headlamp on its high setting while you do all of this. And if it's snowing, leave the tent door open while you're out there doing your business.

2. Manage your stuff. If you have wet clothing items such as socks and shirts, put them on your tentmate's side of the tent. Pro tip: They will dry overnight if you can sneak them into his/her sleeping bag.

3. Fart. Try to eat foods that give you gas, in both quantity and volume, as well as those that produce strange and interesting smells in high intensities. Your tentmate will enjoy periodic breaks from breathing fresh mountain air, as well as trying to come up with words to describe his/her new experiences with the sense of smell. Try: Lentils, textured vegetable protein, other high-fiber foods.

4. Share the warmth. Nothing beats spooning for maximizing bodily warmth. Especially if you're just friends. If your tentmate seems not-so-keen on the idea, explain that it's a common technique used in alpinism, and usually changes nothing in previously platonic relationships. Or say, "Dude, my nose is cold, just let me put it against your neck for a few minutes," or "Come over here, you big teddy bear."

5. Illuminate. Always keep your headlamp on its high beam, which will be helpful for reading your book long after your tentmate has shut off his/her headlamp and gone to sleep. When speaking to your tentmate, make sure to point your headlamp beam directly into his/her eyes.

6. Bring snacks. Who wants to go all the way over to the bear canister to get a midnight snack? Grab a bag of crunchy foods to eat in your sleeping bag, just in case. Corn Nuts, carrots, peanut brittle, and Doritos all make great midnight snacks.

7. Be a good conversationalist. In a tent, you've got a captive audience—and likely a good friend along for the trip—so take advantage. Now's the time to talk about some of your problems, fears, and worries—relationships, digestive issues, and hemorrhoids. Don't you remember being a kid and staying up all night talking and goofing around at someone's slumber party? Why should the fun end just because you're an adult? I mean, really, when you look back on the trip you're not going to talk about all the fun you had sleeping. If your tentmate seems to have dozed off while you're talking to him/her, a friendly "Did you hear that? I think it was a bear," usually gets them re-engaged.

ARE YOU READY FOR YOUR SUMMIT PHOTO?

- ☐ THROW THE HORNS
- ☐ DISPLAY MOUNTAIN CLIMBING GIZMOS
- ☐ JUMP
- ☐ PENSIVELY GAZE INTO THE DISTANCE
- ☐ YOGA POSE
- ☐ CLEVER PROPS

Are you going hiking this weekend? Planning a climb of Mount Hood, Shasta, Rainier? There are two things you should be doing: training, and planning what your summit photo is going to look like. Here are a few things to think about:

1. What are you going to do with your hands?
   a. thumbs up
   b. gang signs
   c. throw the horns
   d. throw the horns and add the extra thumb (which means "I love you" instead of "so metal")
   e. something awkward
   f. shaka
   g. double shaka
   h. hold a pair of coconuts
2. Decide on the mood. Is everyone going to smile? No? Well, are you all going to look tough, like you did in your high school football team photo? Important.
3. Is your helmet crooked?

4. Try to display as much gear as possible so people viewing the photo will know you got into some serious shit up there. Ice axe, trekking poles, headlamp, even if you didn't use any of it—basically empty out your pack and hang everything off your person. Yeah. Now you look like what's-his-name who climbed the Eiger really fast, Ueli Steck, or whatever.

5. Are you jumping? That's cool too, as long as your friend operating the camera can catch you at the top of your trajectory. If not, repeat it as many times as necessary to get the shot. I am not joking, I don't care if you have to jump forty-something times in the thin air above 12,000 feet. Start yelling, "GODAMMIT, JIM" or whatever your friend's name is after the twentieth jump, and then maybe they'll start to get it.

6. It's not a bad idea to have someone take a shot of you by yourself, preferably looking pensive. Do you know how to look pensive? Just gaze away from the camera into the distance and think about some heavy shit, like how many rocks you're standing on (I mean, for real) or whose new baby is going to be your favorite, Kim Kardashian's or Kate Middleton's.

7. Other props: If you bring a beer to the summit, everyone who sees your summit photo will know it was a pretty casual climb for you. If you bring a watermelon, everyone will know you are a badass, and hilarious. Make sure you bring something to cut the watermelon with.

8. Do you do yoga? Now's the time. The only question is which pose. Savasana, Plow Pose, and Happy Baby are always aesthetic and complementary to beautiful backdrops.

FACTS ABOUT CLIMBING MOUNT EVEREST

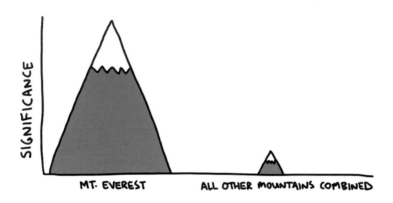

Have you heard of Mount Everest? Mount Everest is the tallest mountain on Earth, so it is also the best mountain on Earth. For several months each year, it is actually the best thing on Earth.

It is so high, its total height is often spoken about in meters, which are a larger unit of measurement than the "feet" used to describe mountains in the United States.

If you ever climb anything, your ultimate goal should be to climb Mount Everest, whether you are a boulderer or a gym climber or someone who just likes to hike up mountains in the summertime.

Mount Everest. Say it again.

The first thing you should know about Mount Everest is that it is expensive. In 2013, total travel, gear, and guiding costs for a summit attempt on Mount Everest are approximately One Shitload of Money. Converted from US dollars into British pounds, the cost is still One Shitload of Money.

Mount Everest is a great place to launch things, from hang gliders, to new brands of XTREME clothing, to awareness campaigns for things people need to know about. If you are unable to get people's attention anywhere else on Earth, you should climb Mount Everest and announce your Important Thing from there. "Everest Base Camp" is the most attention-grabbing dateline in the universe, next to "the White House." If people don't know about caffeine withdrawal headaches yet, it is worth spending a Shitload of Money to go to Mount Everest and let them know.

There are many dangers on Mount Everest, including falling into a crevasse, getting altitude sickness, and death, which is the biggest of the dangers. But it is worth it, because Mount Everest is the best mountain on Earth.

Climbing Mount Everest requires lots of training. Experts recommend climbing a bunch of other—but obviously less significant—mountains on Earth. Especially mountains with lots of snow and ice on them, like Mount Rainier or Mount McKinley. If you can't climb other mountains, you should fill a large backpack with rocks, wrap your head with several pillowcases so it is difficult to breathe, and walk up 3,000 stairs every day. This will get you in shape.

Mount Everest is difficult because (1) it is tall, (2) it is hard to breathe up there, and (3) lots of other people are there. So when there is a good weather window during tourist season, lots of people congregate on the route to the summit (there is only one route). So it is hard to move quickly, kind of like when you try to leave your seat to get to a bathroom during the seventh inning stretch at a Major League Baseball game, or try to switch trains at Grand Central Station during rush hour.

There are dozens of other mountains on Earth, but no one will care if you climb them. If you climb Mount Everest, people will be interested.

Despite the risk of dying from all kinds of things including avalanches and falling off ladders, Mount Everest is a popular and worthy objective for the world's best mountain climbers and lots of other people who are not the world's best mountain climbers. Check it out today. More information is available on the internet.

HOW TO GET YOUR NEW BOYFRIEND/ GIRLFRIEND TO HATE YOUR SPORT

You love snowboarding. Or climbing. Or mountain biking. You've been doing it for so long, you can't remember what your life was like without it. But your new boyfriend/girlfriend doesn't—yet. So you need to teach them. Here are some tips to guarantee they'll never understand you or want to go outdoors with you, and most likely they won't want to date you anymore afterward.

1. Don't start on beginner-level stuff. What, are you supposed to wait around on the bunny slopes, or some birthday-party toprope crag because your new love interest has never skied or climbed before? Pffff. Baptism by fire. Go straight to the Slickrock Trail, fuck the practice loop. You can't even remember what it was like to not be able to climb 5.10s—so start at 5.10, or 5.11.

2. Consider the learning environment. The best time to teach someone how to take down a sport climbing anchor is when they're at the top of the route and you're at the bottom, preferably when there are lots of other people around to listen to you yell instructions. The best place to teach mountain biking techniques is not at the trail-head, but at the steepest spot of singletrack you can find—hopefully in the middle of the day on a Saturday, when other riders can pile up behind your hesitant newbie girlfriend/boyfriend.

3. Get them to buy all the gear before they've tried the sport. Nothing puts the pressure on to learn and immediately love something like spending $2,000 on a bike, or $1,500 on skis plus a season pass. This works the same way that having a baby, or buying a big house, can save a failing marriage.

4. Invite all your friends to accompany the two of you on his/ her first day. Think about it: When you're learning, and having a hard time, nothing beats having six or seven people waiting for you to get down a blue run as you keep falling, or having an audience to perform for when you're already nervous.

5. Remember that their first day is about them experiencing what real climbing, or skiing, or riding, is like—it's not about learning. It's important to have them tag along on something you want to do—your project or your ride. Instead of wasting your time teaching them footwork on a 5.5 toprope route all day, drag them up a multipitch 5.10 with lots of hand and fist jams. Powder day? Perfect! No friends on a powder day, and that includes girlfriends and boyfriends. See you at the bottom, hope you get some face shots, if you know what that means. Also, nothing builds character like a good crash on your first ride.

6. If you can't get them to buy all the gear beforehand, borrow ill-fitting gear for them to try. Nothing beats having a first day with ski boots that are a size too big (even better, a size too small), a climbing helmet that tilts sideways with every move, or a bike that smashes your balls every time you try to step off the frame.

7. Focus on the negative. Your BF doing something right? Ignore it. Point out what he's doing wrong, so he can work on it and suck less. Sigh loudly when you're doing this.

8. Tone is important. When teaching someone something new, be sure to begin all instructions with the word "just," to drive home the point that it's so simple, a two-year-old could do it: so why can't they? Examples:
- "Just put the edge of your shoe on that little dime-sized nub and push off."
- "Just link your turns, like I do. Are you watching me? Just do what I'm doing."
- "Just grab the jug. Just grab it. Just, grab, the jug. Right there. Just grab it."

9. When you get tired of waiting for them, repeat "come on," or "this way," as if you were talking to a dog. You have other shit to do today besides teach them to climb or ride. Let's go. I mean Jeeeeeeesus Christ.

LOSE WEIGHT NOW WITH THE 10,000-FOOT DIET

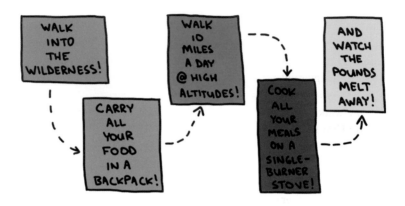

Hey.

Are you sick and tired of diets that JUST DON'T WORK?

Do you feel like a sucker after losing a few pounds with the NEWEST WEIGHT LOSS PRODUCT, but not seeing results after the first few days?

Well, maybe it's time to try a real solution that's guaranteed: THE 10,000-FOOT DIET.

Brought to you by the same people who invented POOPING IN A HOLE IN THE GROUND and SLEEPING ON A ONE-INCH THICK MATTRESS, THE 10,000-FOOT DIET has been proven to work by expedition climbers, long-distance backpackers and thru-hikers, and will work for you.

Listen up, Man-Boobs: Do you have a week of vacation you'd like to dedicate to losing those pesky last few pounds, getting rid of those love handles and that ass-fat, and turning yourself into a shredded, cut, human beast? Forget those surgeries, those meal-replacement bars and shakes, forget meth—THE 10,000-FOOT DIET works, with no adverse side effects.

We'll help you achieve your DREAM BODY with FOUR SIMPLE STEPS:

1. Walk into the wilderness.
2. Carry all your food in a backpack.
3. Walk 10 miles a day at high altitudes.
4. Cook all your meals in a single pot on a one-burner stove.

AND WATCH

THE POUNDS

MELT AWAY

You'll enjoy a breakfast of oatmeal and instant coffee before your lung-busting days of walking with a 40-pound backpack on your back. What's for breakfast the next morning? Certainly not fresh croissants or toasted bagels with cream cheese, with a steaming-hot vanilla latte. No, you'll enjoy another breakfast of oatmeal and instant coffee.

While walking miles and miles of steep terrain all day, you'll snack on Bars That Kind Of Remind You Of Food And Are Pretty Tasty Until You've Eaten Two Every Day For Six Days And Now You're Fuckin Sick Of Them. Mmmm. Atop a mountain somewhere, you may say to your hiking partner, "Wow, these really taste like the chocolate chip cookies my grandmother used to make," and when he or she says, "Really?" You'll reply "Hell, no!" and cackle hysterically.

At dinner, you'll ravenously tear into pasta dishes that taste amazing when you're 15 miles from the nearest road, but are meals even you might have turned your nose up at when you were a drunk college sophomore.

We'll help you lose all that desk-jockey weight in a few short days, or a couple weeks, with something we call MATH:

$$\text{calories consumed} - \text{calories burned} =$$
$$\text{your unwanted pounds disappearing}$$

Who can gain weight when they're burning 6,000 calories a day and only eating 3,000? Certainly not you. Grab your pack, cinch that waist belt around your spare tire, and take our CUSTOM KIND-OF TASTY MEAL PLANS INTO THE BACKCOUNTRY NOW. CALL TODAY.

MAKE PLANS,
NOT RESOLUTIONS

RESOLUTION
RESOLUTION
RESOLUTION
RESOLUTION

In a scene in the spaghetti western *The Good, The Bad and The Ugly*, the One-Armed Bounty Hunter finds Tuco Ramirez in a vulnerable position: in a bubble bath. Pointing his gun at Tuco, he begins a speech: He's been looking for Tuco for eight months, and now he's finally got him where he wants him, and . . . Tuco pulls his gun from beneath the bubbles and shoots the One-Armed Bounty Hunter five times. He stands up in the bathtub and says, "When you have to shoot, shoot. Don't talk."

Every December, we take stock of what we did last year, writing another chapter in our autobiography. A few days later, sometimes after pounding back way too much champagne, we gear up for another trip around the sun by deciding how we want to improve ourselves in the next year. Sometimes we throw out pretty vague statements that don't require us to be accountable to ourselves: I'm going to be a better husband this year. I'm going to lose weight. I'm going to run more.

Every year on his birthday at the end of January, my friend Alan commits to something big for the year. He doesn't hold up a glass of whiskey and announce to his friends that he's going to read fifty-two books, or go to the gym more often. He puts his money where his mouth is and plans something, with a deposit, or plane tickets. The first year, he called Frank Sanders at Devils Tower Climbing and made an appointment to climb the tower with Frank. Then he went and bought a pair of climbing shoes and a pass to a bouldering gym so he could try to figure out how to climb a little bit before they started up the tower in four months. Another year, he put down a $500 deposit on a Grand Teton climb to raise money for a nonprofit. Next year, the Matterhorn. The next year, a trip to the Bugaboos. And so on.

Supposedly, if you write down a goal, you're more likely to achieve it. Is that true if you "write it down" in a Facebook status or a tweet?

I don't know, has anyone ever reminded you of something you said on Facebook? "Hey, Bob, didn't you say six months ago that you were going to climb more/Mt. Rainier/5.12 this year—how's that going?" Right. Somewhere in a billion viral videos, Oatmeal cartoons, George Takei posts, and vacation photo albums, your friends forgot about your New Year's resolution. Did you?

Maybe the question should be: Do we really want to do anything, or do we just want to tell people about it? Business psychologist Peter Shallard says telling people about your next big idea robs you of motivation. You tell people, you reap the rewards of the idea, and then you don't execute.

So are we dreaming, or are we making plans? There's a big difference between broadcasting something about someday riding the Kokopelli Trail and sending one close friend a rough itinerary and asking, What are you doing the weekend of April 20?

I have a handful of people in my life I share some ideas with, and I am careful which ideas, because there is no lag time between me sharing the idea and that person asking me, "When are we doing this?"

In 2009, *The Dirtbag Diaries* published an episode called "The Year of Big Ideas." Fitz [Cahall] interviewed Rangi Smart, a high school math teacher who found a 20-foot constructed jump on one of his favorite mountain bike trails and decided he was going to take a shot at it. He told his wife, then a few friends, and no one shared his stoke. You're an adult, they said, you're providing for a family, et cetera. So he finally told the only people he knew would hold him accountable, to back up his talk: His ninth- and tenth-grade students.

"Once I told my classes—I've got 160 students—and I started making verbal commitments to them," Rangi said, "then it was over. I had to do it."

Rangi told his students because he wanted them to make him feel like he had to hit the jump, not because he wanted them to think he was a rad mountain biker. Then he went out on his own and stuck the landing—barely.

Me, I got a few plans for this year. What are they? Hey, if you have to shoot, shoot.

PLEASE CONTINUE INSTAGRAMMING YOUR AMAZING LIFE

In April, a piece titled "Stop Instagramming Your Perfect Life" started making its way around Facebook and Twitter. The author raised a point that the things our friends post on social media can make us depressed about our own lives—because we only see people's "post-worthy moments": fabulous meals, vacation photos, good experiences. The title of the piece was later changed to "Instagram's Envy Effect," and it was liked on Facebook 145,000-plus times. A quote: "When you're waiting for your coffee to brew, the majority of your friends probably aren't doing anything any more special. But it only takes one friend at the Eiffel Tower to make you feel like a loser."

I wouldn't be the first person to point out that if you're jealous of your friend's life as it looks on Instagram or Facebook, the problem is not social media—it's you.

My Facebook and Instagram feeds are full of friends getting after it, riding mountain bikes, climbing, catching sunsets and sunrises, dawn patrolling, taking their kids out in the outdoors, capturing their dogs looking adorable—in general, finding beauty in everyday life.

Pretty positive stuff, I think. Why would your reaction be to feel bad about yourself when seeing that?

Say your friend Joe has just posted another Instagram photo of a before-work ski run, after-work mountain bike ride, or sunset hike. Is your reaction:

a. *"Joe is always doing something cool. I hate that guy!"*

b. *double-tapping the photo, causing a heart to pop up on your screen*

If you said (a), let me ask you this: If you were having coffee with Joe and he was telling you about his recent vacation, would you listen, nod, and become jealous of him and think about how you disliked Joe because he made you feel bad that you hadn't taken a vacation recently? Or, would you listen and say, "Joe, that sounds really great," and be happy for your friend?

Instagram and Facebook have given us a way to share things instantly, but it should provide more ways for us to be excited for each other, not become more catty and talk shit about our friends. Do you remember life pre-digital sharing? Nobody ever invited you over and said, "Hey, after dinner, I need to show you our photos of the time I got food poisoning and shat my brains out the whole night." Or, "We had a pretty challenging day a couple weeks ago—the kids were being fussy and miserable, crying all through dinner, and Bob and I had a big fight about money. We got most of it on video, want to watch it?"

Are we really comparing our lives to those of our "friends" online? Do we do the same thing in person? After catching up with a friend, do you hang up the phone and say, "I hate her. Her life is so perfect."? Well.

I'm a big fan of social media. I like to know when friends find places that make them feel awesome, or do things they're excited to share, or find joy anywhere. I also like photos of dogs, and there appears to be no oversaturation point of dog photos in my social feeds. I know life is hard and has its ups and downs, and if you want to share those, that's great, too. Please share photos of your new baby, recent trip, day hike, birthday cake, rock climb, sunrise, cute dog, dirty feet, amazing meal, inspiration, and happy moments. I will double-tap that and click "Like," and I will be happy for you just a tiny digital bit.

SOMETIMES YOU GET A HIGH-FIVE FROM THE UNIVERSE

I had about ten minutes before my flight, enough time to grab one more cup of coffee. I had rushed to finish one more assignment on the floor of the Salt Lake City airport before my flight to O'Hare and a somewhat tight connection to Zurich. Just as I was about to order a coffee, I heard a man behind me ask, "Are you Leonard?"

I turned, and a man and his wife stood looking at me, an open passport in his hands. He looked at it, then looked at me, then back at the passport.

"Yes," I said, my mouth dropping. "Wow." I reached out and he handed me the passport, my passport, that I had left on the floor a few hundred yards from the coffee stand. I had hurriedly unplugged my computer from its last North American electrical outlet, packed up my stuff and left my passport, boarding pass inside, sitting next to a potted plant in the busy terminal.

I said, "Thank you," then "Thank you" again, and the guy and his wife smiled and walked on their way. I said thank you ten more times in my head, stuffed my passport and boarding pass back in my backpack, and ordered a coffee, sighing and shaking my head in disbelief that I had left my goddamn passport on the floor of an airport minutes before the start of a three-week work trip.

And that guy had seen it, picked it up, and walked around the terminal for a couple minutes trying to find a guy who looked like the guy in the photo, and handed it to me, no questions asked, no expectation of any reward, just two people doing the right thing on their way to baggage claim. I did my best to communicate my gratitude, but how do you thank someone for saving you from thousands of dollars in airline tickets, days of stress, missed schedules, even identity theft? I should have given him a bear hug right there at the coffee stand.

My friend Mick told me he had a friend who said, "I used to think I was gonna change the world. Now I just let people onto the freeway." I always loved that line, because I think it says something about what people can do to make other people's lives better—all those little things that don't make the evening news.

Most days, I think that most people aren't going to save the world in the way we usually think of that phrase: feed starving children, rescue families from burning homes, start a nonprofit that helps people find a new start.

But then I think about people like that guy who handed me back my passport, or you, when you find someone's wallet at a restaurant and give it to the manager, or pick up a dropped pacifier for someone who's holding a baby and trying to juggle three other things, or let someone in front of you in line at the grocery store when they have two items to buy and you have twenty-five, I think, "Yeah, maybe everyone's going to save the world."

THE PURE JOY
OF FIXIE DAVE

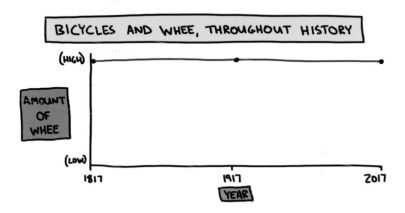

A couple weeks ago at a party, I saw Dave Nice for the first time in a long time. We started talking about the interesting nearby town of Colorado City, Arizona, and he mentioned a restaurant there, saying, "I was dating a girl in Kanab for a little while and I would stop there to eat during my ride over there to see her."

What is notable about this sentence is that each time he went to see this girl, (1) Dave bicycled 62 miles each way, and (2) Dave rides a fixed-gear mountain bike. Dave doesn't drive.

I met Dave back in 2006, while sitting outside a coffee shop in Denver. He had the previous weekend ridden the 68-mile Laramie Enduro mountain bike race, and became the first person ever to finish it on a fixed gear. He had also pedaled his bike to the starting line, 130 miles from Denver, over the two days prior to the race.

Dave and I became friends through the weekly Sunday morning breakfast ride at Salvagetti, and I wrote a couple stories about him for different publications—at the time, he was trying to be the first person to finish the Great Divide Mountain Bike Route on a fixie, which some people thought was crazy, some people thought was ballsy, and some people just realized it was Dave doing what he did: ride his bike.

In 2008, I met him at the same coffee shop to interview him for a story for the *Mountain Gazette*. He walked in the door at St. Mark's with a tremendous sunburn, and I asked him what he had been up to. He said he'd just finished a ride, and listed a half-dozen trails outside of Denver. When I asked, "How long of a ride was that?" Dave said about 160 miles. And here he was, standing next to me ordering a sandwich and a beer like he had just ridden his bike from a few blocks away. I of course asked, "Well, what's the longest ride you've ever done in twenty-four hours?"

"Uh, 276 miles, over five mountain passes in the Front Range—but that was mostly pavement." "Oh, sure, mostly pavement," I said. "What did you do afterward?" "Slept for sixteen hours," he said. Of course you did.

Dave loves all the things you love: good food, beer, bikes. He just loves his bike about a thousand times more than you do.

It had been a long time since I'd seen him, but three minutes into our conversation at that party a few weeks ago, I remembered exactly what it was I liked about talking to Dave: Mid-conversation, I am listening to what he's saying, but I can't hear him over the thoughts popping into my head:

I like my bike, too.

I should ride my bike more.

I would be happier if I rode my bike more.

I am going to ride my bike tomorrow.

Where is my bike? Maybe I should just take it on a spin around the block right now.

This, I think, happens to everyone who knows Dave and likes bicycles. Nobody needs to remind him that he loves his bike. It never gets neglected, never gathers dust anywhere. He rode 16,000-plus miles in 2012, went through eleven chains, and burned through a dozen tires.

Since Dave doesn't drive, a lot of his miles are commuting miles. He told me once a few years ago—when he was wearing cutoff pants and skateboard shoes—that he doesn't wear lycra when he rides because he wants people to see him riding his bike and believe they can do it, that they don't need to buy a bunch of special gear and clothing to ride a bike. I liked that a lot, because that's the way he is: Not some hyper-ripped athlete, just a dude who wants to talk about good beer and good breakfast joints, and, "Hey, we should go ride Gooseberry

Mesa or Buffalo Creek sometime." And then he goes and rides a Century while you're eating dinner, watching TV, and going to bed.

Maybe if you asked, Dave would say he is trying to inspire people a little bit. But I don't think he is. I think he just has a simple but tremendous love for the joy that bikes bring most of us, and he has the courage to make that the central point of his life, not merely a hobby or an accessory.

I like running into Dave, because he reminds me of the things I want more of in my life, but lose focus of every once in awhile. We always try to remind ourselves, Work to Live, Don't Live to Work—and then we catch ourselves stressing over work again and pushing other things to the side to make room for it. Dave lives to ride, and he doesn't need a sticker on his laptop or water bottle to remind him to do it.

WHAT'S THE BEST RAIN JACKET?

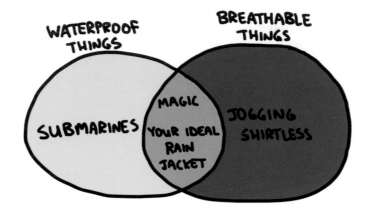

When you're buying a rain jacket, you probably have lots of questions, none of which really matter besides "Which rain jacket is best for me?" Do yourself a favor and stop asking other questions, because if you do ask other questions, you will find yourself sucked into a whirlpool of information preying upon your inability to do math and science as an adult.

You want a jacket that's waterproof and breathable, right? Well.

Lots of smart folks have spent billions of dollars chasing the holy grail of "waterproof breathable," which is an awesome thing and has given us some great products that do a hell of a lot better job of breathing than those of fifteen or twenty years ago. There are several waterproof breathable materials out there, most of which are great. What is hard is verbalizing the difference between Jacket X and Jacket Y, or how waterproof something is compared to the adjacent something on the rack. Turns out there is science and math involved, things many of us have not done since high school or college, so that shit is hard to understand.

But no, really, what's the best rain jacket?

A few years ago, I got an assignment to write an article about waterproof breathable materials. Jesus H. Christ did I feel dumb. I dug through studies, did math, tried to understand it all, and found out neat things: for example, testers use something called a "sweating mannequin" to test the breathability of apparel. Apparently someone has invented a sweating mannequin. I had images of my high school science teachers' faces twisting in disappointment and hurt, maybe anger.

There's RET (resistance to evaporative transfer or resistance of evaporation of a textile, depending on who you ask), also MVT (moisture vapor transmission) or MVTR (moisture vapor transmission rate). All of them are kind of the same thing. At the end of it, I decided a sealed thermoplastic water bottle is waterproof. Jogging shirtless is breathable.

And I also discovered that the best rain jacket is . . . well, REI has put together a great guide to help you decide that very thing. It's called "Rainwear: How It Works," and it's 7,400 words long.

When I worked on the floor at a large outdoor retail store, one of the most common, and difficult-to-answer, questions we'd get was: Is this waterproof? This is not a dumb question.

People would ask that about jackets, GPS units, backpacks, tent flies, sleeping bags, hiking boots, camera cases, watches—everything in the store. And they were justified—usually it's hard to find a roof to stand under when you're in the out-of-doors, so if it rains, some of your stuff is going to get wet. So you want a few waterproof things, or maybe just a Ziploc bag to keep important stuff in like your cell phone and Subway punch card.

If a customer asked about an item that was less waterproof than Gore-Tex, say a tent rainfly or a nylon backpack, we would always say, "It's water resistant."

Which is true. Most things resist water for a little while. Even a slice of Wonder Bread will give your phone some protection from a downpour for a few seconds before it disintegrates. Gore-Tex trail running shoes are waterproof, but only until you step into a 4-inch-deep puddle and water gets into the shoe from the top.

THINGS THAT ARE GENERALLY WATERPROOF	THINGS THAT ARE GENERALLY NOT WATERPROOF
BOATS	BACKPACKS
DRY BAGS	SOFT SHELL
TENTS (PROPERLY SET UP)	NEWSPAPERS
GORE-TEX/eVENT/	COTTON T-SHIRTS
MEMBRAIN/ETC.	SLEEPING BAGS
FISH TANKS	SALTINE CRACKERS

Knowing all this, if I were still a retail shop employee and someone asked me, "Hey, man, what's the best rain jacket?" I would have three possible responses:

1. "Jacket X. Jacket X is the most expensive rain shell we carry, so obviously it is the best."
2. "How much college did you get? You should get more college and then go read about waterproof breathable materials on the internet."
3. "Jacket Y. I wear Jacket Y, and I have climbed literally dozens of mountains; plus I work here, which means I must know something about gear."

A few years after my short career on the sales floor, I met Dustin, my old pal from the shop, to climb a peak in southern Arizona. The night after we climbed, we cooked dinner at a rustic campground near the peak, standing under a ramada made from the wood of saguaro cacti—the roof being one-inch-wide pieces of saguaro wood laid out parallel to each other, with one-inch gaps all along the way.

"Hey, you think this is waterproof?" I asked Dustin as raindrops started to pelt us through the porous roof. Without missing a beat, he deadpanned, "I'd say it's water-resistant."

YOUR BEST VACATION IS SOMEONE'S WORST NIGHTMARE

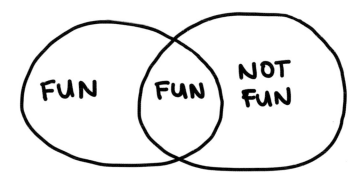

My friend Aaron is a pretty normal guy, by most standards: high school math teacher, homeowner, happily married, good hygiene, pays his bills, et cetera. We see each other several times a year, and almost every time we get together, we talk about one of his recent vacations with his wife, Krista. Without fail, this happens at least once in the conversation:

1. Aaron tells the story about some part of the trip, which includes one or more of the following: altitude sickness or other illness, monsoon rain, equipment failure, freezing cold, high winds, darkness, constipation, the opposite of constipation, saddle sores, mountain storms, and flesh wounds.

2. I listen, while making a face that is half-smiling, half-cringing, wanting to hear more heinous details, but not wanting to hear more. Sometimes I interject things like, "Oh yeah, that's the worst place for a saddle sore," or "Oh, I had that happen with a blue bag one time, too."

3. We shake our heads and laugh.

Aaron doesn't get lost. He doesn't go into things unprepared. But sometimes, when you get halfway around the world, or you're in the wilderness, or on a bike tour, things just happen. These are, as a friend says, the potential side effects of ecstasy. Among all the collateral damage of the vacation, there was a sunset, or a summit, or an opulent meal after hours of near-starvation, or all of those.

I saw a bumper sticker a couple weeks ago that said, "My best vacation is your worst nightmare." I was sure I could have a good conversation with the owner of that car.

Pretend you are Bob. Your co-worker asks you how your vacation was. Pick answer (1) or answer (2):

1. Oh, it was great, Larry. I spent Monday through Friday trying to sleep on a thin pad next to two other people in a 6-foot-wide tent in the snow. We wore 3-pound boots with crampons on them, and by the third day, everyone smelled like a dead deer. We walked uphill on hard snow, uneven rocks, and ice every day and carried 40-pound backpacks. On the fourth day, the sun came out for a few hours, so we woke up at 1 a.m. and walked uphill at high altitude, and at 11 a.m. we turned around and started walking downhill. Oh, the best part is we pooped in blue plastic bags every day and carried the bags of poop in our packs the entire time.

2. Oh, it was great, Larry. I sat on the beach and drank Mai Tais for five days. Got a massage, slept till noon every day. Oh, one day I went snorkeling for a couple hours. It was so relaxing.

Ever notice no one ever uses the word "vacation" when they describe outdoor-centric travel? We substitute "trip." Taking a trip to Yosemite. A trip to Alaska. A trip to Baja. "Vacation" is more like spa, sightsee, relax, recharge, find the perfect balance between sitting and lying down in a chaise lounge somewhere, doze off in the sand—not endo, poop in a bag, get saddle sores, puke from exertion, get gobies from hand-jamming, explore new frontiers in body odor. Isn't it?

I did a fundraising climb on Mount Shasta a couple years ago with my old high school pal Robb, and he told me that he explained to his dad what we were doing—getting up at midnight, et cetera—and his dad, a sensible man, said: "That is the dumbest. Goddamn thing. I have ever heard."

I laughed, because Robb's dad is right. It's absurd what we do for fun sometimes. You could probably say something about the fact that most of us spend fifty weeks a year getting soft behind a desk, and we need visceral experiences to recharge, not more inactivity.

Or you could say people are different—opposites, many times—and in fact, there's a good chance my best vacation is your worst nightmare. Hell, my favorite pizza could be your worst nightmare, and my best mixtape as well. Some of your friends get you, and some don't get you.

Aaron and I disagree on a lot of things, but his definition of fun and vacation is similar to mine, which is maybe why we remain friends after seven years. The first day I met him—actually, the first couple hours—I have this memory of getting my face stung with blowing snow on Flattop Mountain in Rocky Mountain National Park during one of many 40-mph gusts, and Aaron laughing and yelling back to me, "It lets you know you're alive!" Indeed, my friend.

ELEVEN WAYS TO MAKE THAT CHAIRLIFT RIDE AWKWARD

Ski season is here, and you'll be spending anywhere from three to fifteen minutes sharing chairlifts with people you may or may not know. It's enough time to get to know someone a little bit, or have a brief conversation about snow conditions, or how busy or not busy the mountain is.

Or, you can make things very uncomfortable for everyone. Here are a few tips.

1. Repeatedly touch their skis with your skis. People love this, whether you're slightly rubbing your edges on their topsheets, gently resting your skis on top of theirs to take some weight off your legs, or delivering tiny little kicks from your edges to theirs.

2. Talk over everyone. If you're on the far left side of a four-person chair, only talk to the person on the far right side, and vice versa. This works best if you've never met them before the chairlift ride.

3. Pull down the safety bar without warning anyone first.

4. Fart loudly. Farting, loudly, can make almost any situation awkward—first dates, elevator rides, job interviews, et cetera. It can work just as well on a chairlift. Here's the thing, though: You're wearing a lot of layers, so the sound will be kind of muffled. It's a good idea to announce, "That was a fart," immediately after you do it, lest your fellow chairlift riders think it was just the chair going over the rollers on the tower, or some friction between someone's pants and the seat covering.

5. **Talk about your last relationship.** Was it your fault, was it his or her fault . . . who knows? Strangers you've just met are usually a good source of objective advice—they've probably been through a tough breakup or two. It's OK to cry, but flip your goggles up before you get too many tears on the inside of the lens.

6. **Tell them your conspiracy theories**. People deserve to know the truth, whether that's 9/11, the JFK assassination, the Federal Reserve System, or why you got passed over for a promotion at work for that asswipe Gary.

7. **Fall out, but save yourself at the last second.** It's usually good to have a hold of a part of the chairlift with at least one hand before you do this, but if that's not possible, grab someone's boot or pant leg on your way off.

8. **Offer them a pickle, pig's foot, or Vienna sausage from a jar inside your jacket**

9. **In the gondola, ask: "You, guys, don't mind if I smoke some weed, do you?"** Or just do it without asking.

10. **Find a way to talk about your diet.** Are you paleo? Vegan? Vegetarian? Eating a gluten-free diet? Only eating locally grown produce? Getting all the nutrients you need from breathing air? A chairlift is a perfect chance to tell someone about it, and why. Say something like, "So where are you from?" and no matter what they answer (or before they answer), immediately begin describing your current diet. Whether they seem interested or not, try to convince them to adopt your diet too. Not that excited about your diet? Religion and politics are two other great topics to discuss with total strangers.

11. **Ask them on a date.** Doesn't matter if you're not attracted to them, or if they're a man and you normally date women, or if they're a woman and you normally date men, or if their spouse is very obviously sitting next to them. Works best if combined with one of, or all of, the above (time permitting).

DO YOU HAVE OBSESSIVE CAMPFIRE ADJUSTMENT SYNDROME?

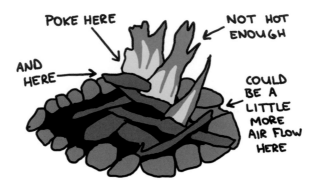

Do you ever stare at a burning pile of logs and find yourself unable to stop futzing with it? Do you look at a campfire and immediately see one or more ways you could improve it? Are you the guy or girl sitting closest to the fire, always wearing a pair of beat-up leather gloves, or holding a narrow piece of split log, so you can adjust the infrastructure according to your next whim?

If you answered "yes" to any of these three questions, you may have Obsessive Campfire Adjustment Syndrome. OCAS affects one out of every four camping enthusiasts in their lifetime, which means you have a 25 percent chance of developing symptoms. It also means that the next time you go camping in a group of four, three of you will enjoy the campfire, contentedly staring into its embers like cave people, but one of you will not stop messing with the goddamn fire.

Ask yourself:

- Are you able to just sit and enjoy a campfire for what it is, a source of light and heat in the dark, cold night? If you answered No, you may have OCAS.

- Do you think you, not the wind, can control the direction that campfire smoke blows? If you answered Yes, you may have OCAS.
- Have you ever put a huge log on the fire, then gone to bed five minutes later, leaving someone else with the responsibility of making sure the fire goes out? This is not a symptom, but it is kind of a dick move, and you should probably stop doing it.

Sufferers of OCAS may not show symptoms until their mid-30s or early 40s. People with OCAS may not know they have OCAS. Symptoms may only surface when someone with OCAS is on a date.

If you suspect a friend may have OCAS, it is your responsibility to confront them. Try saying things like, "Dave, why don't you sit down and stop fucking with the damn fire?"

Talk to your doctor about OCAS today. You're not alone. Many sufferers of OCAS have gone on to enjoy a lifetime of weekend campfires without so much as even adding wood when the fire is about to go out.

Ask your doctor about which OCAS treatment options are right for you. Stop worrying, and start enjoying campfires today. If you have trouble concentrating, or have an erection lasting four hours or more, that probably has nothing to do with OCAS.

DON'T FOCUS ON THE DOG SHIT

"THIS SIDEWALK IS COMPLETELY
COVERED IN DOG SHIT"

☐ = SIDEWALK
◼ = DOG SHIT

In the span of a few minutes yesterday morning, I read about a shotgun-wielding man threatening a neighbor teaching his daughter to ride her bike, watched a GoPro video from a mountain biker in Cape Town getting robbed at gunpoint on a trail, and read a report that the earth is on the brink of a great extinction.

I wondered, What the hell's the point of me recycling my peanut butter jar, or conserving water, or riding my bike instead of driving somewhere? If the world's turning into the kind of place where you can't even teach your kids to ride a bike without getting threatened, I mean, jeez. Especially if it's all on the brink of extinction anyway.

Maybe it's the twenty-four-hour news cycle, or the fact that "if it bleeds, it leads" still guides news, or that internet comments are at most times the absolute rock bottom of human interaction; but it seems some days it's very easy to find negative things out there. Plus traffic, plus deadlines and work, plus bills, plus everything else we have to deal with. Sitting down at a desk is going to kill you, and stress is going to kill you, and breakfast sandwiches are going to kill you, LIFE, my friend, is going to kill you.

When I find myself in a down spot, I remember one of my favorite tweets ever, from @shitmydadsays: "Don't focus on the one guy who hates you. You don't go to the park and set your picnic down next to the only pile of dog shit."

More so the second sentence than the first, that yes, why would you go set up a nice picnic next to a pile of dog shit? Of course many of us do, metaphorically. This sandwich is great, but it would be better if that baby across the room wasn't crying. Sounds like things are going well at work, Bob, but how can I steer this conversation to where we can talk about which political party I think is causing all the world's problems? We channel Eeyore instead of remembering that, as Ed Abbey wrote, "It is an honor and a privilege to be alive, however briefly, on this marvelous planet we call Earth."

I used to read movie reviews in a certain newspaper in order to figure out what I wanted to see, and it seemed like nothing ever impressed a certain writer. This movie was good, but several things were wrong with it, or another movie was funny, but several of the characters were underdeveloped, or one scene was less than believable, or there was this small hole in the plot. After a while, I realized this certain movie critic was making me want to not go see movies. And I like movies. I wanted to write him and ask, "Do you even like movies? It seems like you hate them." I couldn't remember a single movie he had enjoyed. So I stopped reading his, and started reading Roger Ebert's, because that guy loved movies (rest in peace), and when I read his reviews, I wanted to go to a movie.

There are a lot of things wrong with the world. There are eight billion people on the planet, and plenty of terrible things are happening. Maybe those things are legitimate cause for worry, or action, or at least consideration. But sometimes they're only worth consideration, and worrying isn't going to make a bit of difference besides add to your worries in an otherwise pretty good life. Surrounding that one pile of dog shit is a beautiful park with a lot of places to set up your metaphorical picnic.

HIKING IS COOL

Do you ever think hiking doesn't get much respect anymore?

Wait, better question: Remember that hiking film that showed at the Banff Mountain Film Festival, then went viral after all the magazines shared it on Facebook?

Me neither. But hell, a couple weekends ago, I was out on a trail in Rocky Mountain National Park trying to get a photo of a specific rock formation, and I realized I was hiking. Not mountain biking or approaching a rock climb or ice climb, or skiing or snowboarding, or trail running, or really anything above sub-gnar. But it was . . . fun. Fun? Yeah, it was nice.

Fact: Hiking is actually just walking, only on dirt or rocks or other uneven surfaces. Or walking some place where an animal larger than you could possibly show up and kill and eat you.

Yet hiking doesn't get so much love when it has to compete with more XTREME sports in the outdoor realm: even though you can take your shirt off to do it, and it was basically responsible for *Desert Solitaire*, lots of Thoreau's material—and all of John Muir's writing, and thusly the Sierra Club.

Also, just FYI, before you get all arrogant about walking from your house to Starbucks to get a latte, remember that hiking was the predecessor to walking. Because there were no sidewalks when your ancestors were out trying to take down a saber-toothed tiger with a spear. They hiked, then later there were roads and sidewalks for walking, and later, there was Starbucks.

Some other facts about hiking:

- Hiking has been known to increase the satisfaction level of eating many types of freeze-dried food, as well as several flavors of energy bars, up to 35 percent.
- Hiking was the inspiration for skiing and snowshoeing. Actually, the rage induced by postholing while hiking was probably the inspiration for the birth of those two things, but whatever.
- Hiking often happens spontaneously to mountain bikers.
- Unlike other XTREME sports like rock climbing and heli-skiing, you don't need hundreds or thousands of dollars' worth of gadgets and shiny things to hike. If you have shoes, a Snickers bar, and a bottle of water, you can go hiking. Also, if you only have shoes and no Snickers bar or bottle of water, you can still go hiking.
- If you do want to spend a bunch of money on hiking gadgets, you can totally do that too.
- Bears basically spend their entire lives hiking, and bears are rad.
- You can sometimes see bears while you are hiking, which can be good or bad.
- If you have no idea what the hell you're doing or where to go, there are literally dozens of books about hiking. Try googling "hiking books" and you should find a shitload of them.
- Some hikes end at rock climbing destinations, like El Capitan and Castleton Tower. If you are not a rock climber, hikes that do not end at rock climbing destinations will probably be more interesting.
- Most popular hikes are on trails. You do not necessarily need a trail to go hiking. If you don't have a trail, you are "bushwhacking," which is a lot like hiking, but slower and less fun.
- Hikes range in distance from under 100 feet to thousands of miles. If you have never been hiking before, you should start at the lower end of the scale instead of, say, the Pacific Crest Trail, which requires more skills and sometimes entails quitting your job.

If you are interested in fun, or nature, or exercise, or breathtaking views—or all four—there's a good chance you might like hiking. Give it a try today!

INTRODUCING THE HEAVY BACKPACK WORKOUT

THE HEAVY BACKPACK WORKOUT: A STEP-BY-STEP PLAN

STEP 1: GET A HUGE BACKPACK

STEP 2: PUT A BUNCH OF SHIT IN THAT BACKPACK

STEP 3: PUT THE HEAVY BACKPACK ON YOUR BACK

STEP 4: GO FOR A WALK YOU CAN MEASURE IN "MILES" OR "DAYS"

You've tried everything to get in shape: the Shake Weight, BowFlex, FlexBelt, 8 Minute Abs, NordicTrack, P90X (or maybe P12X), Total Gym—and still, you somehow don't have an ass that people can bounce quarters off. What gives?

Maybe you're not eating right. Maybe you're not doing the workouts with enough intensity. Maybe you're confused because magazines tell you to do something different with your training and nutrition every single issue.

OR MAYBE ALL THOSE OTHER WORKOUTS ARE BULLSHIT.

You need a fitness plan that works. Something that will shock your body into the type of fitness that can only be brought about by tricking it into thinking it's the only way to survive.

Not something you can squeeze in with a few minutes a day, in between pulling pans of cookies out of the oven, or in between typing emails. You need something closer to what your ancestors were doing while they were inventing the original Paleo Diet—which they didn't call "the Paleo Diet." They called it, "Hey, I'm Going to Go Get Some Food So All of Us Don't Die." And it required lots of walking and carrying things, which burned a lot more calories than sitting at a desk doing whatever it is we do for fifty hours a week so we can pay for a roof and walls and a 6-foot-wide TV with infinity colors or pixels or whatever.

Do you need all sorts of new equipment, like a heavy club, a spear, and a loincloth made out of the hide of a saber-toothed tiger? Hell no. This workout requires one piece of equipment, and it doesn't even have to be new or comfortable: A backpack.

This is the Heavy Backpack Workout.

It does not cost $1,800, and Chuck Norris and Christie Brinkley will not tell you about it at 1:30 a.m. while you're eating Cheetos on your couch. Its title was not created by a team of brilliant marketers, or even really considered that carefully. But it will chisel you down into being LESS FAT THAN BEFORE YOU STARTED.

So, how does it work?

- Step 1: Get a huge backpack.
- Step 2: Put a bunch of shit in that backpack.
- Step 3: Put the heavy backpack on your back.
- Step 4: Go for a walk you can measure in "miles" or "days."

Your feet will hurt. Your hips and shoulders might hurt. You may experience chafing. You may put photos of yourself doing the Heavy Backpack Workout on Instagram with little inspirational quotes underneath your photo. You may create a hashtag in order to create a sense of community around what you are doing, and encourage others to do the same. After your workout, you may return to civilization and cancel out all your efforts by eating 2,000 calories of bacon cheeseburgers, beer, and milkshakes in one sitting. The important thing is that you keep going out and doing it. Is it getting colder outside? Wear a jacket. Too much snow on the ground? Get a pair of skis or snowshoes. Or simply posthole—it burns more calories.

What phone number do you have to call to find out more about this incredible, game-changing workout? What website do you need to visit for more information? Where can you enter your credit card number to gain access to this revolution? The answer to all these questions is: NONE. (And also "none" and "nowhere," respectively).

Just review steps 1–4 from above and get off your ass and do it. Did you forget the four steps already? Maybe you would like them in a more brief, easily Tweet-able form? Here you go:

Get backpack, fill with stuff, put on back, go walk.

#heavybackpackworkout

IT TURNS OUT YOU *CAN* BUY HAPPINESS

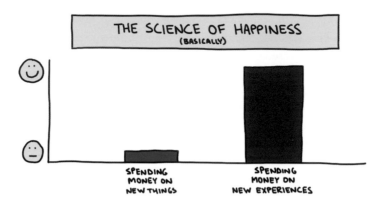

A couple weeks ago, Alastair Humphreys told me about the Explore feature on Kayak.com that allows you to enter the amount of money you'd liked to spend, and shows you where you can fly in the world for that amount.

This is of particular interest to Alastair, because this year he's encouraging everyone to save £20 (or $20, or €20) every week for the entire year, and then take that money and plan an adventure with it—for $1,000. He said at the time of our conversation, a little over halfway through the year, that he would be able to get from his home in the UK to New Zealand, according to Kayak.

I said, "They should show you things you could buy other than that, that won't make you as happy, right next to it—like you could get a bigger TV."

A few weeks later, Alastair challenged readers of his blog to verbalize this exact thing: Would you rather go on a $1,000 adventure, or buy a $1,000 couch?

It's a direct question. Is it an easy answer? Although you're going to get a lot of use out of a couch, I'd personally bet if you spent that money on a trip instead, you'd probably have better memories. I mean, when we're writing out our "here's what we did this past year" holiday cards to everyone, I don't know how many of us include a photo of a piece of furniture we bought.

We always say, "You can't buy happiness," and then we keep trying to do it, getting the next flashy new car so we can sit in traffic in it, or the incrementally better best new smartphone, or the bike costing thousands of dollars and hundreds of man-hours of research and development that we think feels lighter and faster than the one that company made two years ago.

But it turns out you actually can buy happiness, in a way: A study published in August in the journal *Psychological Science* analyzed data on how more than 2,000 people felt about buying experiences versus products. They found that for most people spending money on experiences, not material goods, is more rewarding.

A news release from the Association for Psychological Science said about the study results:

- "To get the most enjoyment out of our dollar, science tells us to focus our discretionary spending on trips over TVs, on concerts over clothing, since experiences tend to bring more enduring pleasure than do material goods."
- "[The researchers] found that people were happier at times when they were thinking about a future experiential purchase than they were at times when they weren't thinking about a purchase at all. There was no relative increase or decrease in happiness when they were thinking about a future material purchase."
- "Students reported positive feelings about both types of purchases, but those who were assigned to think about their impending experiential purchases, such as ski passes or concert tickets, reported their anticipation as more pleasant than those who were assigned to think about impending material purchases, such as clothing and laptops."

Or, as Naavi Singh wrote in an NPR story about the study, "People queue up for days in order to get their hands on the latest iPhone, or what feels like eons for a table at that hip new brunch place. You may be better off spending time and money on the latter."

Of course, you don't need to spend money at all to be happy—but let's be honest: you're going to spend some money on something that you think will be fun this year.

Just FYI, If you have $700 burning a hole in your pocket right now, you can buy:

- The top-of-the-line Roomba vacuum cleaning robot
- A 64GB iPad Air
- A jacket from Anthropologie
- A flight from Denver to Honolulu
- A flight from Denver to the Cayman Islands
- A flight from L.A. to Rome
- A flight from Chicago to Shanghai
- Enough gasoline to drive to Yosemite National Park from almost anywhere in the Lower 48
- A guided climb of Mount Hood

A few of the items on that list will last longer than a couple years.

THE BENEFITS OF DISCOMFORT

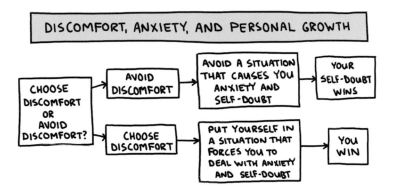

DISCOMFORT, ANXIETY, AND PERSONAL GROWTH

CHOOSE DISCOMFORT OR AVOID DISCOMFORT? → AVOID DISCOMFORT → AVOID A SITUATION THAT CAUSES YOU ANXIETY AND SELF-DOUBT → YOUR SELF-DOUBT WINS

CHOOSE DISCOMFORT → PUT YOURSELF IN A SITUATION THAT FORCES YOU TO DEAL WITH ANXIETY AND SELF-DOUBT → YOU WIN

About a year ago, psychologist and author Kelly McGonigal gave a TED Talk on "How to Make Stress Your Friend," which has now been viewed six million times. To paraphrase, McGonigal said this: Stress can kill you, but only if you believe stress is bad for your health. If you don't believe it's bad for you, stress won't kill you.

Which is quite revolutionary, but it wasn't the part of the talk that I frantically transcribed as I was listening a few weeks ago, then rewound it and listened again to make sure I got it right. After the talk, the host asked McGonigal: How does this apply to people who are, for example, choosing between a stressful job and a non-stressful job? She said:

One thing we know for certain is that chasing meaning is better for your health than trying to avoid discomfort. And so I would say that's really the best way to make decisions, go after what it is that creates meaning in your life and then trust yourself to handle the stress that follows.

In the past century Americans have developed many ways to remove life's discomforts and become more "civilized," and now we can have things like central air conditioning, $3,000 mattresses, and $1,500 reclining chairs. But all along, the pendulum was swinging the other way for people who went back out into the mountains and woods to sleep in the dirt, get sweaty, get rained on, and maybe spend a night shivering and waiting for the sun to come up.

In the adventure world, we see a billion examples of this: climbers who live out of cars for months or years at a time, ordinary people who spend six months thru-hiking the Appalachian Trail or PCT with ultralight packs, others who spend three weeks hauling gear and sitting in tents waiting for a weather window for a summit attempt. And we all have those moments ourselves: whether we're about to puke from the exertion of climbing a thousand feet on a bike or a set of crampons or in a pair of running shoes, or getting blasted in the face with 40-mph-wind-driven snow, or freaking out about falling above a piece of not-so-great gear. We're not doing it so we can get a six-pack or a selfie—we must think there's something else out there.

Cory Richards talks about it in his film *A Tribute to Discomfort*, in which he describes some of the more uncomfortable moments in his photography career, including the avalanche that in 2011 almost buried him on Gasherbrum II. Art Davidson titled his book about the 1967 first winter ascent of Denali *Minus 148 Degrees* for the low temperature the team experienced in what became a battle for survival. Years later he said in an interview, "It's not just about a mountain in winter, but about having a dream, about taking on a great challenge and then struggling as hard as you can to reach your goal—or to survive."

During my adult years learning from people in the adventure community, I've tried to make the uncomfortable (or unsure) choice whenever I can, figuring it worked for lots of people I know, so maybe it'll work for me. When I started writing my first book, I thought of a million different first sentences, but went with the one I thought was the most true: "I don't know if I'm the only one who thinks that when you set out looking for the big answers in life, you gotta be as uncomfortable as possible when you do it."

Lots of people picked up on Kelly McGonigal's quote from that TED Talk. It gives some scientific justification to the uncomfortable choices we make in life, from raising kids (which all parents will tell you is no picnic at first but incredibly meaningful), to quitting our job for a new uncertain one, to climbing mountains. Turns out the path to your dreams is a little scary sometimes.

Later, in a great interview with the We Belong Project, McGonigal went on to say:

> *Avoiding discomfort is the world's worst strategy because it requires choosing discomfort. For example, if you choose to avoid situations that make you anxious, you are choosing anxiety, and strengthening anxiety's ability to control you. If you choose to avoid opportunities that trigger self-doubt, you are choosing self-doubt and convincing self-doubt it is right. . . . Do you want to feel anxiety while avoiding things that have meaning, or do you want to feel anxiety while you do them?*

THE DEFINITION OF ADVENTURE

> "FOR ME, ADVENTURE IS WHEN EVERYTHING GOES WRONG. THAT'S WHEN THE ADVENTURE STARTS."
> — YVON CHOUINARD

> " I GREW UP POOR AND HAD NOTHING. EVERYTHING I DID IN MY LIFE WAS AN ADVENTURE."
> — MY DAD

As I descended the corniced summit ridge, I saw a climber coming up the same path. I hacked out a small ledge in the snow on the uphill side of the path and waved for him to come up and pass. There was not much room for two people, and a fall to either side of the ridge wouldn't stop for 1,000 feet or more.

The Mönch, by most definitions, is a pretty casual climb in the Alps: After a train ride to about 11,300 feet, you walk a snowcat track to the base of a ridge, scramble and climb snow on an exposed ridge to the summit at 13,474 feet. It's not exactly a walk in the park (people have died on it), but it's no Eiger North Face, for sure. You can order a coffee before you start up the ridge, and walk into an Indian restaurant fifteen minutes after you take your crampons off. But the view as you climb up is amazing: jagged, snow-covered peaks as far as you can see to the south, the largest glacier in the Alps starting its weaving, 14-mile descent 5,000 feet below.

As the man approached, he slowed and stopped right in front of me, smiling. I gave him a thumbs up, gestured to the mountains and said, "Beautiful, amazing," hoping he might recognize one English word. He nodded, smiled bigger, and said, "Czech Republic," and I said,

"USA." He slowly pronounced "voon-dah-bah," (*Wunderbar*, which translates as "wonderful") looking around, and we had one German word in common, two guys in helmets and hoods on a knife-edge ridge having a moment together, a little in disbelief that something could be so beautiful. I laughed and nodded. He held his hand up, started to move his feet to continue upward, hand still in the air, and then he did a slight bow as he grabbed my arm and gently squeezed, like he had been climbing all day waiting for someone to share the view with.

I watched him walk away for a second, stepped back into the trench and continued down, unable to remove the shit-eating grin from my face for several minutes, sure that that was the best thing that had happened to me during my entire year of climbing, maybe ever.

One day when I got back, a friend asked on Facebook, "Has the word 'adventure' become cliché?" And I thought about that, and yes, Yvon Chouinard says it's overused, and plenty of people agree with him. And I thought about all the emails in my inbox from friends or acquaintances who have climbed The Nose in a day, soloed remote big walls in faraway countries, and gone on proper "expeditions," where they get dropped off on glaciers for weeks at a time so they can climb or ski mountains nearby, and how I may never get on something worthy of *National Geographic*, or a Goal Zero sponsorship. Sometimes I wonder if I waste too much time comparing my own adventures to those of my friends or peers, in that ridiculous way someone compares their lawn to their neighbors' lawn, or their new car to their coworker's car.

Then I remember that I grew up in a small town in Iowa in the 1990s, and not so long ago, my definition of "adventure" was going to a bar in a different state to get shitfaced. So that's a little perspective.

I interviewed my dad a few years ago for a *Dirtbag Diaries* episode, and the best thing he said during our talk was this: "I grew up poor, and had nothing. Everything I did in my life was an adventure."

That guy from the Czech Republic, on the summit ridge of the Mönch, had probably traveled even less than me to get there. It's a twelve-hour train ride or an eight-hour drive from Prague. He must have been in his mid- to late fifties, and lived most of his life that close to the Alps. But he was so excited to be there.

And I think maybe it's all about gratitude. Is this an adventure, or is that an adventure? If my dad says so, I think it is.

THE HIERARCHY OF CAMPING

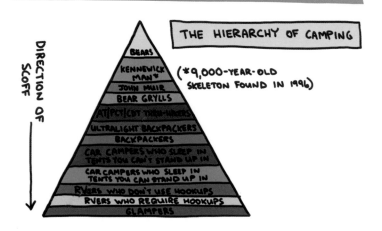

THE HIERARCHY OF CAMPING

DIRECTION OF SCOFF

BEARS

KENNEWICK MAN* (*9,000-YEAR-OLD SKELETON FOUND IN 1996)

JOHN MUIR

BEAR GRYLLS

AT/PCT/CDT THRU-HIKERS

ULTRALIGHT BACKPACKERS

BACKPACKERS

CAR CAMPERS WHO SLEEP IN TENTS YOU CAN'T STAND UP IN

CAR CAMPERS WHO SLEEP IN TENTS YOU CAN STAND UP IN

RVERS WHO DON'T USE HOOKUPS

RVERS WHO REQUIRE HOOKUPS

GLAMPERS

Ever pull up next to someone at a campground and notice they brought way more stuff than you did? Or get to a campsite after hiking 9 or 10 miles and look over to see your friend pulling all kinds of superfluous crap out of his/her backpack?

I mean, camping is roughing it, right? It's supposed to be uncomfortable. It's perfectly natural to feel a little self-righteous when you notice someone has brought what you estimate to be too many creature comforts along: Come on, man, is that an Aeropress in your pack? Who brought the ice cream maker car camping? Whoa whoa whoa, is that a pillow?

Like the food chain, everyone who "goes camping" has a place on the spectrum of roughing it. Above you are people who take fewer comfort items, and below you are all those weenies who apparently can't make it a single night without their down booties/extra-thick camping pad/ butane-powered curling iron/stuffed animal collection.

This is the Hierarchy of Camping. If you sleep outdoors, you are on it. And you look up to someone, unless you are a bear, because you are at the top. Or John Muir or Kennewick Man, because you have been dead for a hundred years or thousands of years, respectively. Your attitude toward those beneath you on the hierarchy is up to you, of course.

UTAHLORADO: AN IDEA FOR A MEGA-STATE OF AWESOMENESS

Dear states of Utah and Colorado:

Hey, so you know what would be cool? If Utah and Colorado became one giant state called "Utahlorado."

I know we've spent a lot of time comparing the two—who has better skiing, who has better climbing, whatever—so obviously the best way to settle it is to merge into a mega-state larger than California, with nine national parks and forty-plus ski areas, adult beer for everyone, legalized marijuana, and fry sauce.

Many great things have started in Colorado, and many great things have started in Utah. Here is a non-exhaustive listing:

Utah	Colorado
Desert Solitaire	The Colorado River
Commercial whitewater rafting	Tommy Caldwell
Aron Ralston's speaking career	The 5Point Film Festival
Wasatch Dawn Patrol	Chipotle Mexican Grill
Butch Cassidy and the Sundance Kid	The Kokopelli Trail
Quesadilla Mobilla	DeVotchKa

Some Utahns might not be so open to things like legalized marijuana, or adult beer, but hey, how about professional baseball, football, and hockey teams, plus the Ouray Ice Park? And of course some Coloradans may not be excited about including a state with a somewhat-less-liberal political ideology in its new border, but how about we smooth that over with Zion National Park and Indian Creek? Yeah, try that hand jam. Doesn't that feel better?

Utah has the Greatest Snow on Earth, which is something to be proud of. It doesn't have Silverton or Wolf Creek. What if it had both? Stop thinking about things in terms of Fruita vs. Moab, or Slickrock/Porcupine Rim/Gooseberry Mesa vs. The 401/Monarch Crest. Think about all of that rolled into the recreation paradise of Utahlorado.

And think about the license plate options: Peyton Manning throwing a football through Delicate Arch? Or maybe the green mountains of Colorado's current license plates, with "UtahloRADo" on them, celebrating the addition of the word "rad" to Utahns' new home state? Maybe Coors could make a new tan can with Bryce Canyon on the front, or the skyline of downtown Salt Lake City? Actually, that might not go over so well. But, hey, musicians covering "Rocky Mountain High" would only have to add one syllable to the chorus, which wouldn't be so awkward. Try it once: "Rocky Mountain High, Utah-loradooooo."

This is an opportunity to bring thousands of miles of hiking and biking trails, tens of thousands of climbing routes, thousands of ski runs, miles and miles of beautiful mountains and incredible desert terrain together inside one contiguous, but also fairly meaningless border, and maybe sell some cool new T-shirts. Think of all those hours you spend staring out your office window, wondering, "Do I like Utah or Colorado better?" Problem solved: You love Utahlorado. And what's not to love? There's something for everyone.

WHAT STORY ARE YOU TELLING YOURSELF?

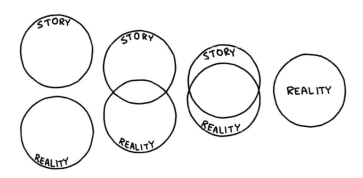

Chad Kellogg died in Patagonia on Valentine's Day in 2014, at age forty-two. I didn't know him very well, just through a handful of phone interviews and one very brief in-person meeting. If you heard anything about Chad, it was probably something about his attempts to break the speed record on Everest—that was the most attention-grabbing thing.

But he was a real climber, an all-around alpinist, and my impression of him was that he had an insanely high level of fitness gained through working harder than anyone out there. He sold all of his stuff and lived at the very edge of bankruptcy to continue to do what he loved: climbing. He did massive traverses and big climbs in the Cascades, put up new routes on big technical peaks in Patagonia, Alaska, Nepal, and China. He was a hero to lots of climbers for his work ethic, his enthusiasm, and his attitude.

I respected Chad, but didn't know so much about him until he died, and his friends started to share stories about him—things he did, things he said, how he climbed in the mountains. I scrolled through a Tumblr page set up by his friends to collect memories of Chad, and I found one by his friend Mark Westman, who knew Chad for seventeen years. My favorite part of Mark's post was this sentence: "When I catch myself in moments of negative self-talk or low self-image, Chad's words of advice he once offered have always brought me back to center: 'The story you tell yourself becomes your reality.'"

I wrote that one down. I doubt Chad would have ever have said so, but the story he kept living and telling himself over years, to me, seemed just short of a being a superhero. Speed record on Rainier. Speed record on Denali. Diagnosed with colon cancer. Beats it. First ascent on huge peak on this side of the globe. First ascent on that side of the globe. He wasn't in climbing films or magazines or ad campaigns—he just went out and did it, in some of the most amazing places in the world.

You might think he had almost nothing in common with John "Slomo" Kitchin, a sixty-nine-year-old man who skates the same stretch of boardwalk on San Diego's Pacific Beach every day. Besides both following their respective bliss, I'd say they couldn't have been less alike. Except one weekend, while watching the *New York Times* documentary on Slomo at the 5Point Film Festival, I heard him say this: "Everybody has the capacity to dream up and believe anything he wants to. The shrinks, or the psychoanalysts, would call it a 'personal delusional system,' and you believe it because you choose to."

Slomo left a successful medical career to devote himself more or less full-time to skating, or as he says, trying to get back to the state of mind he had when he was eleven years old, before he started the trajectory into the middle third of life, when everything got too serious. If you watch the film, you can see everyone on the Pacific Beach boardwalk react with joy to what they see as a man doing exactly what he wants with his life. I watch Slomo, and I'm a little envious of the simplicity of his bliss and the courage it took for him to pursue it.

Both Chad and Slomo were/are living very unique lives of infectious enthusiasm, and both were clearly in charge of their own stories. Chad didn't believe he was a general contractor; he believed he was a mountain climber. Slomo understood he had been working just for the material ends, and becoming, in his words, "an asshole"—and that's not what he wanted to be; so he moved into a studio apartment and concentrated on skating on the boardwalk. It seems Chad and Slomo were kind of saying the same thing, that you are whoever you think you are, if you believe it. Maybe we should all take a step back and ask: what story am I telling myself?

TEN TIPS TO HELP LIGHTEN YOUR BACKPACK

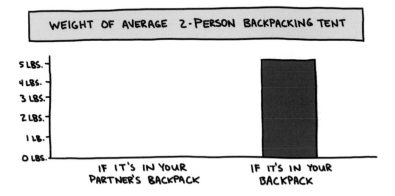

WEIGHT OF AVERAGE 2-PERSON BACKPACKING TENT

5 LBS.
4 LBS.
3 LBS.
2 LBS.
1 LB.
0 LBS.

IF IT'S IN YOUR PARTNER'S BACKPACK

IF IT'S IN YOUR BACKPACK

A heavy backpack can make a backpacking trip no fun at all. Here are a few tips to lighten your load and maximize the fun on your next outing:

1. Instead of packing eight beers for your overnight backpacking trip, just take six. Total weight savings: 1.5 pounds.
2. At the trailhead, open your pack and remove two or three pairs of shoes from it. Leave them in the car.
3. Instead of that old kerosene lantern, try a headlamp. This can shave several ounces off your pack weight. For example, by leaving your Coleman 1 Mantle Kerosene Lantern at home and replacing it with a Petzl Tikka headlamp, you'll decrease your total pack weight by 4 pounds, 11 ounces.
4. If you notice you have a baby with you, run back into town quick and find someone to babysit it for the weekend. Babies are heavy and become awkward to carry after several miles. Plus they require lots of extra food and gear like diapers.

5. At the trailhead, set aside all your heavy stuff and ask your friend to carry it for you. Explain that you are trying to lighten your pack.

6. Try to limit yourself to three or fewer stuffed animals.

7. Portable video game consoles are heavy. Instead of your Playstation Vita (1 pound, 10 ounces), download a few games like Angry Birds, Star Wars II, 80 Days, Asphalt 8, and NBA Jam to your iPhone and hope those will get you by for the weekend or week.

8. Instead of packing separate bottles of shampoo, conditioner, mousse, gel, detangler, and hairspray, try using a stylish but lightweight hat to hide your dirty hair for the weekend.

9. Buy all new stuff. If your stuff is from last year, it's very likely way heavier than this year's stuff. Go into a gear store and tell them to give you all new camping stuff, and enjoy the weight savings, plus the shiny newness. If anyone gives you any shit about it, such as your spouse, tell them your old stuff was too heavy and it was giving you back pain.

10. If you have some things that are troubling you, tell them to someone on the way to your hike, or to your friend when you meet at the trailhead. Even if it's just a convenience store attendant or bartender, it can be very cathartic to get your problems off your chest. This will lighten your pack, if only metaphysically.

THIRTEEN PIECES OF GEAR EVERY ALL-AROUND ADVENTURER SHOULD HAVE

Normally I use this space to talk about not buying a bunch of shiny new gear, to sarcastically review entire categories of gear, or to extol the virtues of old, crappy bicycles. In a departure from that, I wanted to do something that might genuinely help people. So if you want to get started doing things in the outdoors but don't know where to begin buying gear, here are a few things I'd put on my shopping list if I were starting all over again at zero gear. Hopefully it will help you sort through all that stuff in the gear store and guide you to what you really need to get started. Obviously gear companies would love to have you buy everything they sell, but truthfully, a good foundation of stuff can get you going on plenty of adventures. Lots of these things can be found used on eBay or at gear consignment shops.

Note: This blog (and my adventures) are supported by Vasque and Outdoor Research, so I'm obviously biased towards their products. But I'm not getting paid to list anyone's products on this page. This is just stuff that has worked for me.

1. THIRTY-LITER BACKPACK

A 30-liter pack is a good size for lots of single-day activities—day hikes, ski resort days, peak bagging, hauling books/laptops to the office or across campus, bike commuting, picnicking—whatever. If you're a sport climber, you should probably be able to fit all your stuff for a day at the crag in a 30-liter pack, and if you're a savvy trad climber, same deal (unless you're carrying a No. 4 and No. 5 Camalot). Maybe you'll have to put the rope on the outside of your pack. But in general, if you're buying one backpack for all your one-day activities, 30 liters is a great size. A bajillion people make 30-liter packs (or 28-liter, or 32-liter), and you can find them all over the internet. For years, I've used a Wild Things Guide Pack, which is probably at the high end of the price range, but it's light, minimalist, and can take a major beating.

2. LIGHTWEIGHT SOFT SHELL JACKET

A solid lightweight, breathable soft shell jacket should be a go-to layer for spring and summer (or high-altitude) mountain bike rides, trail runs, multipitch rock climbs, peak bagging, day hikes, or anything where you might get a stiff cool breeze when you're a little sweaty, or get exposed to some wind and possibly a little rain. Since 2011, I have carried the same jacket (actually, the same model of jacket, but I've gone through a few, especially after I zipped one up in a dry suit and finally ripped it) for all these activities—the Outdoor Research Ferrosi Hoody. I'm sure lots of other companies sell something similar to it—it's a very thin soft shell hooded jacket (side rant: never buy a jacket without a hood) that weighs a little less than 14 ounces and packs down small enough to fit in the lid of any backpack. I've found dozens of times that the difference between shivering at a belay and being just warm enough is the ability to pull a jacket hood up over my helmeted head. I realize you don't often need a hooded jacket while mountain biking or bike commuting, but come on, I'm not going to buy a separate, non-hooded jacket just to wear on my bike—this one will do just fine.

3. SIXTY-LITER BACKPACK

A 60-liter pack isn't the biggest you can buy, but most of us aren't going on backpacking trips longer than seven days often enough to justify owning anything much bigger than that. I think 60 liters is perfect for three- or four-day trips when you want to pack into heavy, multiday climbs of peaks like Mount Shasta or Mount Rainier, as a piece of checked luggage for most things I do (which don't often—actually, ever—involve clothes on hangers), seven-day backpacking trips when you don't want to be carrying a bunch of extra crap anyway, and days of extreme luxury at the climbing crag. You should get a pack that fits you first and worry about features later (in my opinion), but a couple packs I've liked over the past couple years are the Deuter ACT Zero 50 + 15 (super-light) and the Osprey Atmos AG 65 (super comfy, but I don't own one—I just got to borrow one for a three-day trip once).

4. HEADLAMP

If you go camping, backpacking, need to find things under your fridge, do car repairs on the street in front of your apartment, have permanently shut off your car's interior light because of your tendency to leave it on and find a dead battery the next time you try to start your car, a headlamp is for you. You can spend $400 on one that will illuminate a mountain bike trail at 20 mph (useful for those times you find yourself needing lighting while traveling at high speeds), or you can spend $19.95 and get a basic one from Petzl, Black Diamond, or Princeton Tec (useful for everything but lighting while traveling at high speeds). I've always preferred simple, minimalist lights that run on small batteries and don't light up a million yards away from you or have a bunch of functions that you have to tap Morse codes on the power button to operate. If I was a search and rescue volunteer or a caver, I might prefer something a little more powerful, but really, for most folks, basic headlamps are just fine (my opinion). The only times they've ever let me down are a handful of episodes of rappelling into the dark when I really would have liked to see my rope ends hanging 115 feet down into the dark (but didn't absolutely need to).

I had a Princeton Tec EOS that I used religiously for five years until the case finally cracked (but it still works, and I still keep it in my van as a backup), and I've recently been using a Black Diamond ReVolt that I dig for the ability to lock the on/off button, and because I can recharge it on a USB instead of using all those AAA batteries. I know people hate to carry extra shit in the backcountry, but I never leave the trailhead without a headlamp stuffed in my pack somewhere, and that's prevented a few nights of sitting on a rock in the dark waiting for the sun to come up again.

5. MSR DROMEDARY

It's a big, tough, bag that holds a ton of water. That's handy when you're backpacking or bike touring and need to carry a gallon with you to camp a few miles from your last water source, or knowing that you can just fill it up so you don't have to keep walking down to a lake or creek to fill up a cooking pot. You can even blow it up and use it as a pillow at night if you want. It collapses down to almost nothing. You can get a thing to turn it into a hydration bladder. Really. It's a big bag of water. I take one water bottle backpacking, and a 4-liter one of these.

6. WATER BOTTLES

To paraphrase Ian MacKaye, companies are not selling you water; they're selling you a plastic bottle. Water is free. If you have a water bottle, you can access and store water so you can take it with you when you walk away from the source, such as an airport drinking fountain. With a full water bottle or two, you have some chance of actually staying hydrated on a trans-Atlantic flight, since you don't have to rely on flight attendants pouring you a 4-ounce cup of bottled water every three hours. I have been using a Klean Kanteen Classic 40-ounce bottle for almost everything, and a Camelbak Podium bottle for running and biking. They work, and have probably saved me from using about a million or so Dasani bottles.

7. TRAIL RUNNING SHOES

Something they don't tell you about running shoes: You can just walk in them if you don't want to run. In fact, it's often less strenuous than running. You can wear trail running shoes for hiking and back-packing, as long as you can live without the ankle support and stout outsole of hiking boots. You can also use trail running shoes to run on surfaces other than trails. I wouldn't stop anyone from buying a pair of hiking boots; but if you've only got room for one pair of outdoor shoes in your luggage, trail running shoes are probably more versatile. I've been wearing the Vasque Pendulum II for the past year, and love their lightweight, not-overbuilt, construction.

8. RAIN SHELL

If you go out there, you're going to get rained on sometime. Which rain jacket is the right one for you? I have two I rely on regularly. The first is the Outdoor Research Helium II, a lightweight shell that packs down to the size of a peanut butter sandwich, and I carry it for bike commuting, mountain biking, day hikes, and multipitch rock climbs in the late spring, summer, and early fall. It's kind of a "just-in-case-it-rains" jacket. For longer trips, or in colder conditions, or with wetter forecasts, I have used the Outdoor Research Axiom (high end of the price spectrum) or Foray Jacket (middle-of-the-road price). Even if you're not planning on a ton of rain, a rain shell can be a great wind-blocking layer for activities when you're spending lots of time exposed to windchill—summer multipitch or alpine rock climbs, fall and spring bike commuting or mountain biking, peak bagging, et cetera.

9. PUFFY JACKET

Pros: super-warm, compresses down to nothing in your backpack, can be used as a pillow. Cons: rips easily, doesn't insulate when wet (unless it's synthetic insulation or treated down), easily perforated by flying sparks from campfires. Be good to your puffy jacket and it will be good to you. It's like an appetizer for the later, full meal of getting into your sleeping bag. It can be your happy place. I have always used small amounts of Krazy Glue to patch the little holes in my puffy jackets, but most people use duct tape. I like the Outdoor Research Transcendent Hoody, which is more of a down-sweater-weight jacket than the kind you'd buy for Mount Rainier, but it's perfect for all the colder-weather spring and summer nights and mornings I have in the desert and in the mountains in the summer.

10. TWO-PERSON BACKPACKING TENT

If you want to buy a bunch of tents for all your needs, you could get a one-person tent for all your solo backpacking (or bikepacking) trips, a two-person tent for trips you take with a friend, a big car-camping tent for weekends with friends when you want to spread out all your stuff and maybe just stand up inside your tent because you can. Or you could just buy a basic two-person backpacking tent and use it for everything—including not taking up as much space as three separate tents in your gear closet/garage. I still own an older version of MSR's Hubba Hubba that I got in 2007, and have recently been impressed with Big Agnes's Copper Spur UL2, but they're both pretty high-end. If you're looking to spend a little less, REI has sold about a million Half Dome 2 tents over the past decade, and it's still under $200.

11. FIFTEEN-DEGREE SLEEPING BAG

I've done most of my camping and backpacking in the past decade in the mountains and deserts in the West, and I've never found a 15-degree sleeping bag to be overkill, and only in rare, way-late-season situations has it proven to be too chilly. If you're a very cold sleeper or are planning on winter camping, a bag with a rating closer to zero degrees is probably more appropriate, but I would say most people buy something moderate (15- or 20-degree rating) and then buy a different sleeping bag for winter so they're not hauling around the extra weight or heat of a winter bag all year. A 15- or 20-degree sleeping bag is a great all-purpose, three-season sleeping bag.

Down sleeping bags are more compressible and lighter but generally more expensive, and synthetic bags are bulkier but have traditionally held insulating value better when wet. But lots of companies are now using treated down, which has helped down insulate better when wet (and dry more quickly than untreated down). I haven't had a ton of experiences where my sleeping bag has been completely saturated, but have been very impressed with treated down in situations of extreme condensation (sleeping without a tent next to a river or another humid scenario) and picking up moisture from the inside of a wet tent or from wet clothes and gear during a rainy trip. I've been using the Big Agnes Bellyache Mountain 17 for a couple years now and remain pretty happy with it.

12. SLEEPING PAD

For sleeping on the ground. They're not all the same, but they're all better than sleeping on the actual ground. I can't 100 percent recommend one particular model for super-cushy unpuncturable comfort, but I've never carried one that weighs more than a pound and a half.

13. ISOBUTANE (CANISTER FUEL) STOVE

Yes, Jetboils are exciting, efficient and compact, but I think a solid (non-Jetboil) canister stove is a great entry point for anyone who's getting started in the outdoors. I like Jetboils for certain applications, but cooking non-dehydrated meals in a pot is not one of them. If you want to make your own pasta, grab a simple canister stove and a windscreen (if it doesn't come with one, make one out of a foil turkey roasting pan from the grocery store) and get going. There are a bajillion models out there. I prefer the slightly-less-than-minimalist ones that stand on their own instead of perching on top of the fuel canister, like the MSR WindPro II—although my most recent purchase was an MSR WhisperLite Universal because the WindPro II was out of stock for a while.

ANATOMY OF A SANDBAG

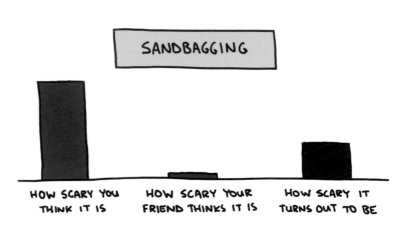

SANDBAGGING

HOW SCARY YOU THINK IT IS   HOW SCARY YOUR FRIEND THINKS IT IS   HOW SCARY IT TURNS OUT TO BE

We all have that friend who may need a little encouraging to do something they're a little apprehensive about or something they're just flat-out scared of. Like leading a run-out pitch, or dropping into a couloir they haven't skied before, or rowing a rapid with a reputation for flipping boats, or riding a technical trail famous for breaking bicycles and bones. Many times, we are that friend who needs the encouraging.

Sometimes, the encouraging requires a tool called "sandbagging," in which one friend convinces an apprehensive friend to do that thing which scares them by making the thing seem easier than it really is. It is not quite lying, but not quite telling the truth either; and in the end, one friend is satisfied that he/she helped the apprehensive friend "push their limits" and the formerly apprehensive friend is . . . well, the reactions vary, really.

Sandbagging occurs when two friends have a different perception of the less-experienced friend's ability, and the more-experienced friend wants to the less-experienced friend to explore their personal capabilities through a formative experience. Sandbagging can be, at one end of the spectrum, challenging, and at the other end, terrifying and deeply emotionally damaging. Here's how it often works.

STAGE 1: DOUBT

Friend 1 believes his/her ability in a sport is not sufficient for a certain objective (example: riding the Portal Trail, leading the crux pitch of *The Naked Edge*, rowing Lava Falls). Friend 2 believes Friend 1's ability is sufficient, and all that's really missing is confidence.

STAGE 2: THE SALES PITCH

This is where Friend 2 tries to supply the appropriate confidence, with a number of tactics to convince Friend 1 that the impossible is possible. Friend 2 minimizes the danger and uncertainty, saying things like "Just relax," "There's a short technical section but other than that, it's easy," "You don't need a No. 4 Camalot for this pitch," "If you can follow it, you can lead it," and many other phrases, usually including the Ultimate Sandbag Axiom, which is, "You'll be fine." The key here is to push the sale, carefully, but firmly.

STAGE 3: COMMITMENT

When Friend 2 says "You'll be fine," Friend 1 only needs to believe it 51 percent. They need just enough confidence to perform The Thing Which They Need But May Not Think They Want: to rack up and tie into the rope, clip into his/her pedals and drop in, grab the oars and pull the boat into the current, buy the plane tickets, or make whatever irreversible first step is necessary for a memorable and formative experience. Friend 2 either needs (a) only a 70 to 80 percent belief that their friend can do The Thing Which They Need But May Not Think They Want, or (b) only a 49 percent belief that they need to remain friends with Friend 1 after the climb.

STAGE 4: THE OUTCOME

After Friend 1 decides to step into the void, march in the direction of their fear, or launch themselves into the often terrifying river of personal growth, a number of outcomes are possible, both positive and negative. Unscientific estimates put the success rate of a sand-bagging in the 75 percent realm, but are only anecdotal. In the case of sandbag failure, negative outcomes such as broken bones, broken bicycle components, swearing off climbing for the rest of one's life, and embarrassing public breakups are possible. (It's important to note here that sandbagging in romantic relationships is extremely risky, often disastrous, and should be attempted only with extreme caution, if at all.) On the positive side, personal limits are often shattered, climbing careers are begun, Facebook profile photos are captured, and astronomical leaps in personal growth can occur.

Sometimes, although not always, a friendship will survive a sandbag. The odds of this vary widely based on many factors, including the age of the friendship, the audaciousness of the sandbag, the respective emotional stability of the two friends involved, each person's appreciation of the value of intense experiences, and the amount of physical and emotional damage incurred by the outcome of the sandbag. It's important to weigh these factors to the best of your ability before you actually sandbag a close friend.

A good general rule is: If your friend does not survive your sandbag, your friendship will not survive it either.

BACKPACKING
IS SEXY

Hey, girl.

Or guy. I want you to know something about that hobby of yours that you partake in from two to two hundred days a year.

It's sexy.

Yes, I'm talking about backpacking.

The way you suffer up a steep trail with forty pounds of stuff in your backpack is hot, in the same sexy sports-sort-of-way as beach volleyball or shirtless rock climbing.

Yeah.

It's in those odd-shaped sweat marks temporarily staining your synthetic fabric shirt when you take your backpack off for a break to drink water and eat room temperature snacks so you can backpack some more. What kind of sandwich is that you're unwrapping?

I like peanut butter and jelly too, baby. Let's eat and keep backpacking all night long.

Oh, you would like to find a place to camp before night falls? I suppose that's a good idea.

I just meant I like to take it slow. With you. Backpacking. Not like those people who trail run or mountain bike—no baby, I like it at three miles per hour, or even one mile an hour if your particular trail gains more than one thousand feet in a mile. Yeah.

FYI, these sturdy yet sensual legs go all the way up to the point where my zip-off pants turn into shorts.

Can I tell you something? I have a bit of a foot fetish. But only for feet bedazzled with fragments of dirt and patches of moleskin. Perhaps you would like to slowly remove the gaiters you're wearing with those hiking shorts and show me yours?

I'm sorry, was that too forward? Maybe we could back up a little. To the part where I build you a roaring but not ostentatious campfire and read to you from my favorite USGS quadrangle map while we sip from a very small bottle of whiskey I rationalized bringing even though I spent the night before weighing all the other items in my pack with a luggage scale.

And then maybe I can get closer to you and your synthetic shirt that never quite loses that specific B.O. smell in its armpits no matter how you washed it since your last hike, and your sleeping bag that holds and beautifully blends the body smells of all your hard work on the trail, plus whatever happened in your digestive tract after we ate that freeze-dried Himalayan Lentils meal from a bag the night before.

I'm sorry. Am I getting you a little hot? As hot as the back sweat you produce while hauling a 45-pound pack up a 2,000-foot climb? Or maybe as hot as the friction between your hips and a too-tightly-cinched waist belt on an old backpack?

I thought that might be the case. I'll just leave this here and you can call me when you're ready to spend a weekend grunting and sweating with a relative stranger, up a long, long trail that feels like it's never going to end.

Just to be clear, I am still talking about backpacking.

Love,
Tony B. Trail Magic

HERE IS A LIST OF FUN THINGS YOU CAN DO ON YOUR BICYCLE

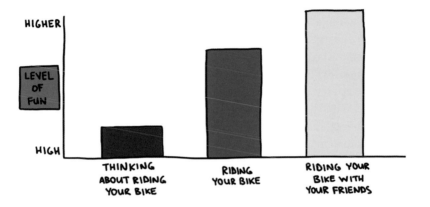

1. Jump it off something.
2. Put foot pegs on the back and give a friend a ride.
3. Ride to a bar with a friend to get a beer.
4. Ride to another bar with a friend to get another beer.
5. Stop riding it to bars before you've had too many beers, and/or ride it somewhere with a friend to get a taco.
6. Tell your friend about how much you love it because of a few specific things like mustache bars or specific geometry or the amount of travel in the fork or the wheel diameter and at the end of your short speech, say, "Do you want to ride it? You should, it's awesome. Go ahead."
7. Clear your head.
8. Enjoy going fast.
9. Enjoy going slow.
10. Ride it up hills and enjoy the pain it causes because you are getting strong or because you are imagining the giant cheeseburger you're going to eat afterward or because it feels good to feel

something after sitting at a desk all day or because it helps you forget about your breakup or your bank account or whatever.

11. Drink a whole shitload of coffee and ride down hills in the dark.
12. "Ride it off a ramp into a large body of water." (Chris Reichel)
13. Do a wheelie.
14. Ride it to your local bike shop, where you hang out and talk to other customers and mechanics about how much you all love bikes.
15. Ride it to work and practice saying "wheeeee" on your commute instead of "goddammit, I hate traffic."
16. Put a small stereo on it and rock out.
17. Put a large stereo on it and rock out.
18. Strap all your stuff to it and ride it across the country.
19. Strap all your stuff to it and ride it across the state.
20. Strap all your stuff to it and ride to the nearest campground.
21. Ride it to a skate park and try to do some cool shit with it.
22. Or just watch the skate park kids do some cool shit.
23. Find a mountain bike trail described as "swoopy" and ride it.
24. Find a mountain bike trail described as "technical" and try to ride it; possibly secretly enjoying picking scabs all next week.
25. Ride with a whole bunch of people, which is either a "parade" or a "gang," depending on your aggressiveness and how many small children are riding with you.
26. Put on a bunch of fancy aerodynamic clothing and ride the hell out of your bike until you're really tired.
27. Don't put on a bunch of fancy aerodynamic clothing but ride the hell out of your bike until you're really tired.
28. Ride with no hands.
29. Ride with no clothes on.
30. Ride your bike somewhere practical like the grocery store or coffee shop and enjoy not having to park a car when you get there.
31. Try a new thing (wider bars, single speed, different wheel diameter size, fully rigid, full suspension, fatbike, fixie) and realize *this* is what you've been waiting for your whole life, holy shit, let me tell you, seriously.
32. Ride it somewhere without calling it a "workout," or using Strava, or a heart-rate monitor.
33. Or do all that stuff, you know, whatever your thing is.

34. Unclip your foot from your SPDs well before you stop so you don't eat shit at a stoplight.
35. Have a good idea while pedaling and thinking about nothing in particular.
36. Enjoy the 360-degree view you have while riding, and congratulate yourself on saving thousands of dollars by not buying a convertible to get that same view.
37. Get on it right now (or in an hour, or after work) and ride it instead of wishing you were riding it.

HOW TO BE A TERRIBLE ADVENTURE PARTNER

RELATIONSHIP OF BAD ADVENTURE PARTNERS AND STUFF

- ■ FORGETS STUFF
- ■ WAITS UNTIL LAST MINUTE TO PACK STUFF
- ■ BRINGS UNPREPARED STUFF
- ■ BREAKS YOUR STUFF
- ■ KEEPS YOUR STUFF AFTER

Sometimes when you invite a new friend out skiing, biking, climbing, or backpacking, it goes really well. But maybe during the course of the day or trip, you get the feeling you'd like to not ski or bike or climb or hike with that person ever again. In that case, you can ignore their phone calls, graciously deflect their requests to hang out, or flat-out tell them you'd rather just be non-active friends and keep the relationship to activities like drinking beer and eating nachos.

Or, you can sabotage the whole deal by being a complete shitbag of a partner. Here are some techniques to help you do that:

THE DAY BEFORE

Make vague plans. Give bad directions to your house or the trailhead. Don't discuss who's bringing what communal gear (tent, rack, rope, et cetera). Verbalize all times with the suffix "-ish," giving you plenty of leeway to show up at, say, 7:45, when you planned to meet at "7-ish."

Drink a whole bunch. Drink a lot of beer or hard liquor the night before so you can, in the words of Arlo Guthrie, look and feel your best. A hangover is a good start, but if possible, try to eat combinations of food and booze that have a good chance of making you vomit or racking you with diarrhea the next morning. Example: Jägermeister, followed by something fried (and possibly served on a stick) at 2:30 a.m. If you can't find anything fried on a stick, go get something off the 7-Eleven roller grill. I heard Ueli Steck lived off that kind of stuff.

THE DAY OF

Oversleep. Example: Your friend says, "I'll pick you up at 7 a.m." Set your alarm clock for 6:45 a.m. and hit the snooze button at least once. Or, don't set an alarm at all, and wait for your friend's 7:05 a.m. phone call to rouse you. Then say, "I'll be out in a second, I just have to eat some breakfast, make coffee, brush my teeth, and grab my stuff."

Pack your gear the morning of. This increases your chances of forgetting crucial things like a harness, rain jacket, and food and water. You know where everything is in your house, right? And it's impeccably organized, so you basically only need five minutes to get all your stuff together, no matter what sport we're talking about.

Don't pack food. As soon as you get into your friend's car, announce that you need to "get something to eat." Have them run you by a place that serves breakfast burritos/sandwiches and coffee and get some breakfast. Better yet, have them stop the car twice—once for breakfast, and once for coffee.

After breakfast, announce a second (or third) stop, in which you will run into a grocery store "real quick" to get some food for the hike/bike ride/climb. Alternately, don't do this, and wait until you're a good ways into the trail or approach and ask your friend, "Did you bring any food and water? Could I have some?"

Don't prepare your stuff. Do not check your bike tires or chain the night before—wait until you get to the trailhead and your friend is astride his/her bike waiting for you. Then say, "I just need to pump up my tires. And lube my chain." If you're climbing, keep the rack unorganized so when you pull it out of your pack, it's a big ball of tangled metal. In backcountry skiing, it's always cool to realize the batteries in your beacon are dead exactly as your partner clicks into his/her skis.

Forget some stuff. Climbing? Don't pack the rope. Or the rack. Skiing? Forget your ski pass, or beacon. Biking? Forget the only pair of shoes that work with your SPDs. Most importantly, forget your wallet so your friend has to pay for beers and burgers afterward.

Break their stuff. It's fun for everyone when you can find a way to ski over the back of your friend's skis, especially if they're new, or just intermittently knock your edges up against theirs in the lift line. You can also rip their tent or inexplicably melt a hole in it, or just flat-out fall into it and break a pole or two when you get up to go to the bathroom in the middle of the night. When climbing, everyone gets a cam or a nut stuck from time to time, but leave several hundred dollars of your partner's pieces in the rock throughout a route and they'll never forget you. Especially if you get to the belay and subtly put the blame on them: "Man, you really wedged those things in there."

THE DAY AFTER

Keep some of their stuff. If you're climbing, absentmindedly keep a couple of your partner's cams in the bottom of your pack when you're sorting gear, and discover it when you get home. Also works with bike pumps, tire levers, or other bike tools. This can be especially memorable if you figure out you kept some of their stuff after you've gotten off a plane to somewhere halfway across the country or globe.

Put some bad photos of them on Facebook and/or Instagram. And tag them. And make sure you only post photos of yourself where you're looking really good.

HOW TO BE NICE TO PEOPLE

PEOPLE IN THE WORLD (APPROXIMATE)	HOW MANY JERKS IT TAKES TO RUIN IT FOR EVERYONE (ACCORDING TO MY DAD)

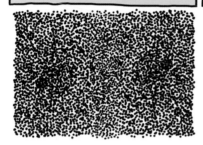

A few weeks ago, I was coasting in my van down Sixth Avenue in Denver, a dollar in my hand ready to hand out the window to whoever was standing with a cardboard sign at the corner of 6th and Colorado (there's always someone there). As I got close, I saw the light was green, and I had to keep moving, and the person had turned their back anyway since traffic was now flying by at 25 mph.

I started to turn left onto Colorado, and the SUV next to me turned left as well, cutting me off. It's not a double turn lane, and they were technically wrong. Immediately I thought, that's not right, and honked my horn. Then I held the horn longer, just to drive home the message in case they hadn't noticed.

I felt embarrassed immediately, that I had gone from wanting to help someone to basically whining in the span of about ten seconds. Stop being an asshole, I said to myself. It wasn't dangerous, I barely had to hit the brakes to avoid them, my day wasn't ruined—the extra-long horn honk was just a way of saying "You're doing it wrong." Like a jerk would say it, though.

Do you ever catch yourself being an asshole? In the car, on the internet, to a barista who misunderstood your order, to a person who disagrees with your political views?

I'm in the middle of what John "Slomo" Kitchin calls "trying to get to the end of my life without becoming an asshole."

But it's hard. We all have things we want to do, not enough time to do them, and the world moves way too slowly when we're at work and not fast enough when we're outside the office. Every once in a while, someone in a grocery store checkout aisle looks back and says, "Hey, you only have one item, why don't you go in front of me?" but usually, everyone is just kind of in our way. We live in a country where we believe it's always Us vs. Them, as if our political parties are two football teams and only one is going to win the Super Bowl of Quality of Life. We don't see any way to work together; we just want our team to win.

In an article near the end of 2014, *Slate* called it "The Year of Outrage." In the story, writer Choire Sicha explained one way we're becoming more angry: "We used to yell at the TV but it couldn't hear us. Finally someone can. So you turn to all the people next to you, all the friends and followers, and you are typing and then you are hitting send, post, tweet, submit."

I wouldn't be the first person to point out that the internet has given us the capability to be incredibly mean to each other, often anonymously. It has, and it seems there are people out there whose sole contribution to the universe is a mass of negative comments about everything, which they work at on a daily basis. We've somehow forgotten that the world does not get better when we say something shitty about someone else, whether one person or a thousand agrees with us. We argue with each other about things we know we'll never budge on, in the end only affirming our belief that the other person is still wrong and we're still right, and our disbelief that they could be such an idiot.

Being nice to people is incredibly simple—google "the Golden Rule" if you need a refresher—but somehow, we've forgotten how to do it.

There are thousands of different paths to happiness, and hundreds of books citing thousands of studies on how to be happy. My own informal, unscientific, study of people I've met who appear to be pretty happy has shown that not being a jerk to other people is as good as any of them.

Here's one very simple example of how not to be a jerk: You are drinking a coffee at a sidewalk cafe and someone walks down the street wearing pants that are way too tight (or way too loose, or too bright or too dark or too short or too long, or basically just different than the pants you're wearing). The way you were brought up, you would never wear those pants. Everyone in your social circle would agree that those pants are too tight. They go against everything you've ever been taught or learned about the world. They're an abomination. How dare that person wear pants that tight.

You could say something to the person next to you, or take a photo and put it on Instagram with a mean comment, or silently shake your head in disgust as the person walks by, or find a social media outlet to communicate a sweeping generalization about people who wear tight pants.

Or you could take control of your own suffering, remind yourself that no one is making you stare at the pants, and really, in the end, that person's tight pants make no difference in your life. Just keep enjoying your coffee and move on with your day.

Better yet, send your mother a text message and ask how she is doing. Or hold the door for the person behind you, or go ahead and let that person who drove all the way to the front before merging just go ahead, or say "thank you" more times in a day than you say "screw you," or choose to look at photos of golden retrievers on Instagram instead of arguing with a Facebook friend who disagrees with you. Because being an asshole never made anybody happy.

PROFESSIONAL GEAR REVIEW: SPOON

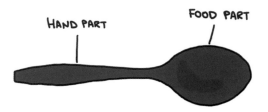

THE INCREDIBLE SPOON
PRETTY STRAIGHTFORWARD, REALLY

HAND PART

FOOD PART

"Perfection is achieved, not when there is nothing more to add, but when there is nothing left to take away."
—Antoine de Saint-Exupéry

After years of rigorous, exhaustively documented testing in both the backcountry and the frontcountry, I feel confident in stating that the spoon is the most superior eating utensil ever created. Yes, you've probably read a similarly superlative statement in a review of a baselayer top or a pair of socks, so let's turn on our bullshit-o-meters and give this some thought.

Check it out: it's a tiny shovel for your face. After a blizzard, when you want to get dozens of cubic feet of snow off your driveway, do you go out there with a pitchfork, a pair of pool cues, or a shovel? That's right. The spoon, even better than a fork or chopsticks, is the most efficient method of moving food into your mouth in the backcountry. After a long day of walking, hiking, climbing, or whatever exercise you prefer to do on dirt or rocks, you want to get food out of that cooking pot and into your digestive system, preferably quickly. You use a spoon.

Oh, you use a spork? I mean, to each their own, but sporks are kind of the futon of the eating utensil world, don't you think? It tries to be two things at once, and does both jobs pretty poorly. Instead of taking a fork and a spoon, you take a spork, and voila, you have a crappy fork and a crappy spoon, all in one. Unless you're talking about the type of spork that is a fork on one end and a spoon on the other end—those work better, but still have fork problems. Like when you accidentally break a tine off the fork, thereby decreasing its carrying capacity by 25 percent. That blows. It's pretty hard to break a spoon.

Maybe you have a titanium spork, or a titanium fork-and-spoon set. It's your money. Have you ever, just before a trip, realized you don't know where your super special camping eating utensil is, and frantically searched your house for it? You own lots of spoons. Calm the fuck down and go grab one out of the drawer in the kitchen. Problem solved. It probably only weighs a few grams more than the missing one anyway.

I think it's safe to say that the spoon did for eating what the camming unit did for traditional rock climbing. Before spoons, we ate with our hands, which is messy, especially when you get spaghetti sauce in your cuticles. Human beings improve the smartphone every few months, but the spoon has been the same for thousands of years. That's perfection.

Yeah, you say, but I can't eat noodles with a spoon. Yes you can. Have you ever put an 8-foot-long tree branch in a campfire? Oh, you did, but you broke it into two to four pieces first? Good call. Do that with your fettuccine or udon before cooking it and our friend the spoon will have no problem moving them from your bowl to your mouth. Or, you know, take something easier to pack and easier to fit in a camping pot, like fusilli, macaroni, penne, rice, couscous . . . you get the idea. If you break up those noodles before cooking, your spoon works just like a fork. Do you want to spread peanut butter on a tortilla? Your spoon works as a knife—a butter knife. It handles soup with ease, and in a pinch, it can be used to move water out of shallow desert potholes into your water bottle.

Your spoon will never turn against you. It's almost impossible to turn a spoon into a weapon, unless you want to spend eight hours sharpening it on a rock. A fork, though? A fork, in the wrong hands, will do some major damage. Just ask that lady who stabbed that other lady for taking the last rib at the barbecue back in May.

Respect your spoon, appreciate it, and it will fill you u_ ' let you down.

Full disclosure: This spoon was not provided to me for free for review purposes. I paid $1.00 retail for it at REI.

SHOUT OUT TO OLD BIKES

BICYCLES AND MAXIMUM JOY CAPABILITY

MAXIMUM JOY PRODUCED

∞

0

BRAND-NEW BIKE   OLD BIKE

A couple Saturdays ago, I got this email from my friend Lee:

> *Would you or anybody else you know be interested in this classic Trek 820 that Kerry rescued from a dumpster? It is in good shape and mechanically looks and feels sound. Seat tube is 56 cm. Seven speed triple. The pedals are mine. Free to a good home. I want my garage back.*

I grabbed two beers out of my fridge to make a down payment on a new-to-me bicycle (total cost: four beers), drove to Lee's house, picked it up, and a few hours later, cruised it over to a friend's house for dinner. Lee had put on new rear brake pads, and the frame has a bunch of dings and scrapes, and the headset was a little loose, but overall, it rides wonderfully. If Lee and I weren't such good friends, I might have even given him up to $150 for it. From what I can tell via some internet research, it's a 1994.

I have not ridden very many new bikes in my life, but I have ridden plenty of old bikes. And this one, well, it's another one of those. A purple one. I believe it retailed for about $300 when I was a freshman in high school, and there's something very satisfying about riding a two-decades-old bike that still works just fine. Especially one your friend's wife found in a dumpster and you bought for four beers.

We've made a billion technological advances to bikes in the past 125 years, making them way lighter, way faster, and more expensive than a year's tuition at a public university. All that stuff is cool, but sometimes we forget that whether it's a carbon/titanium sculpture we can lift with our pinky or a clunky pile of cheap steel we could use for CrossFit workouts, the bicycle is still the most efficient human-powered transportation ever created. And pretty goddamn fun to ride over to the ice cream shop on a summer evening.

As far as the joy of riding to the ice cream shop goes, all those technological advances of the past, say, thirty years don't make much of a difference when you're not trying to be king of the mountain.

Now, there is nothing wrong with riding a nice bicycle. But if you can't enjoy riding a crappy bike, I would go as far as to say that maybe you don't like bikes.

Crappy old bikes are everywhere—pawn shops, thrift stores, garage sales, dumpsters, Craigslist—and many are in better condition than cars built in the same year. Here's a secret: Many people buy bikes and never ride them more than a handful of times, and fifteen or twenty years after the price tags were removed, those bikes are sitting in someone's garage under a layer of dust. Sometimes all those bikes need is a new chain and a basic tune up and they're ready to roll. Sometimes they need a new front wheel because Junior plowed the family SUV into the trash can and pinned the bike behind it on his first time backing out of the garage, but wheels aren't hard to come by. Sometimes the only thing worth saving is the frame, and you can learn almost everything you need to know about bikes spending a handful of nights swapping out the parts for new ones.

Money can buy a lot of things, but there are a lot of things you don't need much of it to buy—including an old bike with a story.

THE TWELVE TYPES OF BIKE COMMUTERS

Everyone knows there are two kinds of people in this world, but did you know there are twelve types of bike commuters? That's right. Here they are. You might be, or have been, or know someone who is, one of them. Or more of them at once. Or maybe there are more than twelve types.

APPREHENSIVE NEOPHYTE

- Pedals onward despite visible terror
- Will evolve to other type of bike commuter after fifteen to twenty more bike commutes

RIGHTEOUS INDIGNATIUS

- Commute has higher purpose than the standard just-getting-to-work utilitarianism. It is for fitness, for environmental reasons, possibly for enlightenment, for avoidance of psychological fatigue that comes from driving in traffic every day. Still, this type is every once in a while affected by traffic or individual drivers who try to kill him/her, and must scream or give finger to cabbie/pizza delivery driver/texting driver drifting into bike lane.

THE OUTLAW

- Aggressively breaks traffic laws
- Gets pissed when motorists make similar infractions
- Fuck you
- And you
- So angry

NO BAD WEATHER, ONLY BAD CLOTHING

- Uses fenders
- Does not look at weather forecast to determine whether today is an OK day to ride to work; only looks at weather forecast to determine clothing strategy
- Fatbikes to work in blizzard
- "Dave, are you sure you wouldn't like a ride home from work today? I mean, it's RAINING out there!"

APPRECIATION AND REAL FEAR OF DEATH

- "Just riding my bike over here, please don't hit me."
- Never has dead batteries in blinking taillight
- Possibly wears reflective vest
- Never rides without helmet

ONE-TIME

- Rode bicycle to office once
- Left bicycle locked to rack in parking garage or in front of building forever
- Bicycle still there, dying slow death with two flat tires, also possibly slowly being stripped of parts

UPS/FEDEX TRUCK DRIVING BIKE COMMUTER

- Doesn't actually ride bicycles, just uses bike lane for parking spot whenever possible
- I'll just put my flashers on.

NYC RESTAURANT DELIVERY GUY

- Somehow goes 22 mph without pedaling
- Never heard of e-bikes

NOT A CYCLIST, JUST GUY RIDING BIKE AROUND CITY

- Would never ride a bike if he had a car/enough money to ride the bus
- Not sure what the big deal is
- Rides in regular clothes

BIKE COP

- Is police officer
- Rides police-issue mountain bike
- Has gun
- Rides on sidewalk
- Is actually at work on bicycle, as opposed to riding to work

DUI GUY/GIRL

- Bikes only because of suspended license
- Flipped-up drop bars
- Sometimes smokes while riding

DRUNK GUY/GIRL

- Bikes only to/from bar
- Sometimes forgets bike at bar
- But isn't DUI Guy/Girl, see, because not driving to bar

THE DAWN WALL
AND THE IDEA OF
"WASTING TIME"

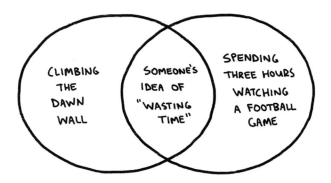

In January 2015, two guys finished climbing an astronomically difficult 3,000-foot route on El Capitan as the world kept up via seemingly every mainstream news source: CNN, the *New York Times*, the *Washington Post, Sports Illustrated,* and all of the major news networks. Climbers and non-climbers followed the final pitches of Kevin Jorgeson and Tommy Caldwell's nineteen-day efforts on a live video feed, which was simultaneously kind of boring (as watching rock climbing from a distance usually is) and absolutely enthralling.

When Jorgeson joined Caldwell at the final anchor at the top of the final pitch, two tired guys hugged at the end of a monumental, multi-year effort, many of us rejoiced, and social media feeds blew up with everyone's own version of "[insert exclamatory phrase here] Dawn Wall!"

Throughout the two weeks of media coverage, a few people seemed to not get the whole thing, calling the climbers adrenaline junkies, or accusing them of doing it for fame or attention or money, or saying that they should have spent their time doing something that would benefit humanity. I dug into the comments section on a

New York Times story on the climb and found a gold mine of vitriol. I cringed, laughed, and collected it and put it all together in an *Adventure Journal* post.

It's one thing to not understand climbing—it turns out it's incredibly complicated to explain why the route, and climb, was such a big deal. If you don't climb, you might not get that the sport of climbing is statistically relatively safe (compared to driving on the freeway), relatively not harmful to the park (compared to the impact of thousands of park visitors every year), and that there are differences between aid climbing, free climbing, and free soloing. Likewise, many of us don't understand the technicalities rules of lots of Olympic sports, or stock car racing, or the categories at the Oscars, and the idea of using or not using ropes in climbing was definitely lost on many people.

But there were also dozens of indignant comments from people who seemed to think the whole thing was a giant waste of time:

Robert Frodeman, Denton, TX
Strikes me as a dumb way to spend one's time. Dangerous, and for what purpose? A thrill. One should devote such considerable energies to something more constructive.

KittyKitty7555, New Jersey
Am I the only one who thinks that the energy directed into this very difficult climb could have been better directed elsewhere? Yes, I'm sure it was really hard, but what was produced except self promotion?

Sometimes we complain that the news is all negative: if-it-bleeds-it-leads, "Man Shot," "Baby Drowns," "Car Accident Kills Six," "Hostage Beheaded," "War Continues Even If We Don't Call It War." And then a story that's hard to see as negative ("Two Men Climb Giant Difficult Rock Face, No One Dies, Some Fingertip Skin Damaged") takes over some headlines for a while and people flock to the internet to take a shit on it, saying these two guys could have done something different with their time.

Well, ok, what's an acceptable way to spend your time, instead of climbing the Dawn Wall? Would it make us feel better to see Tommy Caldwell and Kevin Jorgeson sitting next to us in traffic on Monday morning? Should they have sat down and watched all the seasons of *Game of Thrones* consecutively? Spent some days at one of those drink-wine-while-you-learn-to-paint classes? Done their part to contribute to the three billion hours we spend playing video games each week? Maybe they could have replied to all the internet comments concerning their climb?

When we see someone doing something we deem foolish, we have a tendency to say something like "they have too much time on their hands." And we forget that we're privileged to have any spare time on our hands at all, something that was an unforeseeable luxury not too many generations ago—when we spent all of our time trying to survive—and something that doesn't exist at all for the often-invisible people sometimes halfway around the world who pick the produce we eat or make the clothes we wear.

The advance of civilization has given people the opportunity to have spare time, and with that spare time we have found ways to express ourselves. Art, whether it's Shakespeare or Picasso or Illmatic, or *The Tonight Show With Jimmy Fallon*, is created by people with spare time, and consumed by a much larger amount of people with spare time. Some of it we embrace, some of it we discard, and all of it, in the grand scheme of things, is arguably folly.

Charlie Todd, the founder of the prank collective Improv Everywhere, gave a TED Talk on "The Shared Experience of Absurdity" in 2011, and addressed the criticism he'd heard about how he chose to spend his spare time:

> One of the most common criticisms I see of Improv Everywhere left anonymously on YouTube comments is: 'These people have too much time on their hands.' And you know, not everybody's going to like everything you do, and I've certainly developed a thick skin thanks to internet comments, but that one's always bothered me, because we don't have too much time on our hands. The participants at Improv Everywhere events have just as much leisure time as any other New Yorkers, they just occasionally choose to spend it in an unusual way.
>
> You know, every Saturday and Sunday, hundreds of thousands of people each fall gather in football stadiums to watch games. And I've never seen anybody comment, looking at a football game, saying, 'All those people in the stands, they have too much time on their hands.' And of course they don't. It's a perfectly wonderful

way to spent a weekend afternoon, watching a football game in a stadium. But I think it's also a perfectly valid way to spend an afternoon freezing in place with 200 people in the Grand Central Terminal or dressing up like a Ghostbuster and running through the New York Public Library. . . .

As kids, we're taught to play. And we're never given a reason why we should play. It's just acceptable that play is a good thing. . . . I think, as adults, we need to learn that there's no right or wrong way to play.

In our early years, like Charlie Todd says, we all find different ways to have fun: playground football, drama club, being the class clown, building elaborate models out of toothpicks, rock climbing, writing stories. Some people find ways to turn "play" into a job later, but not all of us do, and some of us consider ourselves lucky enough to hang onto playing well into adulthood as something we can do for a few hours a week or a month.

In an interview with the *New York Times* at the top of El Cap, Jorgeson said, "I hope it inspires people to find their own Dawn Wall." I like to think he means a couple things with that: that we all should have and hold onto big dreams, and we should never stop playing, whether or not everyone agrees that it's making the world a better place.

THE POWER OF A FEAR-BASED FITNESS PLAN

Have you ever committed to something you weren't sure you could do, and then found yourself in the best shape of your life the week before that something happened?

Maybe you signed up for a triathlon, a marathon, an ultramarathon, a twenty-four hour mountain bike race; or you told everyone in your Facebook feed you were going to climb Mount Rainier, or The Nose; or you got a bunch of friends to come spot you while you attempted the hardest boulder problem of your life; or you decided you were going to try to climb forty pitches for your fortieth birthday, or some other foolish thing like that. The Thing.

And then shortly after, you realized, holy shit, now I have to do this. I call this Commitment Remorse. It's like buyer's remorse, but instead of having less money and a purchase you're not even sure you want, you have to start training. Also, unlike buyer's remorse, which tends to disappear in a day or two, Commitment Remorse lasts up until the day of The Thing.

Deep down in your heart, you know that you are not ready for whatever The Thing is. You are a little too fat, or a little too weak, or haven't run or biked or hiked that far in a really long time, or there's dust on top of your fingerboard. You have sandbagged *yourself*. Thankfully, you have some time to get ready through training—and if you don't, as my friend Alan says, "People will arrive either rested or ready. And we'll be rested."

If you have time to train, it is as if someone has lit that proverbial fire under your ass, isn't it? Two weeks ago, you didn't have time to train, and now you make time. You stop binge-watching Netflix and instead drag your ass out to run laps, or get to the climbing gym, or whatever. You dig deep and eat vegetables. You dig even deeper and set your alarm clock for 5 a.m. so you can do the things that you hope will get you ready for The Thing.

Or, you wake up in the middle of the night and stare at the ceiling, wondering if you can do it, The Thing. Maybe you should just call it off, and bail. But people are counting on you. Or you spent a bunch of money on a registration fee, or on the gear to do The Thing. No, no, you can do it. You just need to keep training and eating right. Right? Maybe not. You roll over. Why can't you sleep? Hell, if you can't sleep, you might as well get up and do some cardio or pushups or lunges or something. So you do.

A few weeks or days before The Thing, you are looking pretty good, aren't you? That stuff threatening to turn into a double chin is gone, you can see your hip bones a little bit, and wait—is that an ab? It is! You could not quite scrub laundry on that stomach, but there are signs of ab muscles. Four of them! What a change. How did this happen?

Terror, that's how. Fear of failure at The Thing. Of sucking, and wasting everyone's time and your own money, and maybe some plane tickets. Why does Mount Rainier, or your 5.12b project, or the triathlon, or the ultra, work so much better than those other general objectives like "lose some weight," "get in shape for bikini season," or "look good for my wedding"?

Because unlike the disinterested glances of fellow beachgoers, unlike your own "I've-lost-a-couple-pounds-haven't-I" inspections in the bathroom mirror, unlike your non-judgmental wedding guests, Mount Rainier will crush you. So will the triathlon, or that boulder problem. These things do not care if you "got busy at work" and didn't have time to train, or that you "tried to work out more," and they will not, like your understanding friend, tell you that your half-ass gym attendance looks like it's kind of paying off. The Thing will call your bullshit, and you know it.

You committed to The Thing because you know all of this is true, and it is the only way to trick yourself into getting fit. Sometime after it, there will be another Thing, and after that, another one. And in between those Things, there will be too much ice cream and beer and tacos and Netflix. Something has to motivate you to commit to the next big Thing, right?

TEN WAYS TO TALK ABOUT POWDER SKIING

ON YOUR DEATHBED

TELLING YOUR GRANDKIDS

TELLING YOUR KIDS ABOUT IT

FIVE YEARS LATER

ONE YEAR LATER

NEXT OFF-SEASON

NEXT DAY AT THE OFFICE

IN THE PUB 3 HRS LATER

THAT DAY

HOW MUCH SNOW WAS THERE ON YOUR POWDER DAY?

(A CHART)

Ski season is here. With any luck, you'll have one or more powder days, and they will be the best ski days of your entire season. How should you share the joy of all that snow with the people you know, you love, or you just want to impress? Here are a few ideas.

1. **Be vague, yet hyperbolic.** When you're telling someone who wasn't there about your powder day, say, "Dave. It was so good. You DON'T EVEN KNOW. Dave. It was SO GOOD."

2. **Use gestures.** Hold your hand, palm facing upward, and slap the outside of your leg at the corresponding height of the highest point you believe aerated snow struck you during a run (mid-calf, knee, mid-thigh, hip, rib cage, etc.) Do it hard enough to leave a bruise.

3. **Use hearsay.** "There was so much snow, I heard a guy from [insert name of often-maligned state here] quit after one run and complained that there was 'too much snow' and 'you couldn't even ski in it.'"

4. **Talk about sacrifices you and your friends made to stay out skiing.** Maybe you waited ten minutes to three hours for the first chair. Maybe you didn't even eat lunch. Maybe you, not wanting to take even a five-minute break from slaying pow, soiled yourself midday or even mid-run. Maybe you drove your car into a ditch on the way to the mountain and chose to walk the rest of the way instead of calling for a tow truck. Maybe you quit your job because it was worth it to you for one powder day. Maybe you broke out of a maximum security prison to get there. Maybe it took you ten years to get home after the fall of Troy and your beautiful wife Penelope waited for you faithfully the whole time while rejecting the advances of unruly suitors. Maybe you paid $175 for a lift ticket at Vail, plus parking.

5. **Exaggerate.** For example, "It was so deep, the ski patrol wouldn't let you get on the chairlift with skis that were less than 120 underfoot."

5a. "It was so good, my friend Eric literally drowned in pow. I mean, he died. On the lift line under Chair 8. I could have gone back up to look for him, but sorry, that's just how seriously I take powder days. Sorry, Eric."

6. "Dave. SO GOOD. SO. GOOD. Dave."

7. **Use a social media platform to communicate any of the above items.** I believe Snapchat is the hot shit these days.

8. **Make vomiting noises when describing your powder day.** "It was SO SICK. BLEAAAHHHHHH!!!!!"

9. **Actually vomit.** Just like 8, but wetter.

TWELVE WAYS TO MAKE FRIENDS AT THE CAMPGROUND

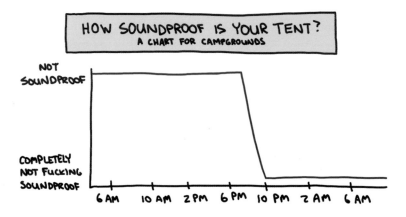

It's summer. Which means it's camping season. Which means you've got a great opportunity to get into nature and meet new friends at a campground somewhere. Here are a few tips to fast-track your way to instant friendship:

1. Arm your car alarm just in case someone tries to break into it or steal it while you're sleeping next to it. Or in case some animal accidentally bumps it, or a gust of wind buffets it exactly right, or something else that's not a car thief causes it to go off at 3 a.m.

2. Grab a beer and head over to the neighboring campsite to chat with your new friends over there about politics. If they don't want to talk politics, try changing the subject to religion. If they don't want to talk about politics or religion, try to find something else to disagree with them about.

3. If your dog is very vocal, territorial, or nervous, and likes to bark throughout the night for these or other reasons, bring him or her along. If you don't have a dog, just bark on your

own between midnight and 5 a.m.—most people can't tell the difference between a dog bark and a human bark that early in the morning.

4. If you leave your campsite to go hiking, fishing, or exploring during the day, leave some snacks out on a picnic table for our animal friends. Squirrels and birds love to chew through wrappers and bags, so snack mix, potato chips, or crackers are always a good choice. If you're in an area where bears are known to congregate, a plate of salmon or other fish is always a nice gesture. Try placing the fish on the dashboard of your car and leaving a window cracked for the bears.

5. Arrive at the campground at 11 p.m. or later. Take a couple laps around the campground searching for the perfect remaining campsite. Use your high-beam headlights to most effectively inspect the campsites from your moving car.

6. After you've found the perfect campsite, set up your stuff, start a campfire, and start drinking with your friends. Sit far enough away from each other that you have to project your voice.

7. Enjoy your campfire and conversation until 2 a.m. or 3 a.m.

8. As you set up your campsite after 11 p.m., make sure to open and close your car doors every time you get another item out of your car. Make sure you slam the door shut—you want to be sure it's closed.

9. Don't be afraid to use your gas-powered generator between the hours of 11 p.m. and 6 a.m. if you need to. If it's too loud for you to sleep, bring a long extension cord so you can put it a ways from your RV.

10. Play some music on a stereo. You like your music, so everyone else probably will, too.

11. Take some wet wood to burn in your campfire, to maximize smoke coverage of the entire campground.

12. Help yourself to your neighbor's cooler of beer, preferably in the middle of your conversation/diatribe about politics or religion. Tell them you will pay them back, even if you have no beer at your campsite.

FIVE STEPS TO ORDERING A PERFECT COFFEE— EVERY TIME

1. **Go into a coffee shop.** Approach the counter, greet the barista and clearly and concisely state your order. Say please and thank you. Put a $1 tip in the tip jar assuming that the barista will really nail it.

2. **Wait patiently.**

3. **When your drink is finished,** collect it from the barista and say thank you.

4. **Choose a place to sit.** Place your coffee drink on the table. Get comfortable. Take a deep breath and look out the window. Think about all the things that are going right with your life, and focus on those instead of worrying about all the stuff you have to do and all the other things that are causing you anxiety but have a 95 percent chance of never happening. Consider the fact that you just paid someone to make coffee for you, which probably means you are in a financial position to feel like you have at least $4 in disposable income. Sure, it could go to your 401k, but potential security and comfort later does

not taste as good as coffee now. And if you do have $4 in disposable income and can spend it on something as frivolous as coffee—because come on, for all your posturing about "needing" coffee and how you're a monster without it, you could probably make it a day or two without it and not stab someone—you have to admit, you're doing pretty well. You're not, for example, $4 short on your rent this month, and you don't owe that money to someone who might break your legs if you don't get it to them by Friday, and you feel perfectly comfortable spending that $4 on a nonessential drink instead of your next meal—you must be pretty confident you'll eat if you're putting that money towards coffee.

So yeah, things are going pretty good, you might go ahead and say to yourself as you sit there in the coffee shop with your Americano, or cappuccino, or latte, or whatever it is you paid that skilled person behind the counter to make for you. Yes, you might have a little pressure with work deadlines, or worry about some potential health issues, which is really just the most immediate fear of death that we all think about from time to time—but we're all dying, aren't we—and you're likely not going to die before you finish your coffee, so it's nice to sit and enjoy that coffee and the few minutes you've taken to sit down and gaze out the window and think about what a nice day it is out there. Or, it's raining, and you're thinking about how nice it is to have a roof over your head right now, instead of standing out in it waiting for a bus or changing a flat tire on the side of the freeway. You're probably in a pretty safe place, in that coffee shop, very likely a spot on Earth that is not randomly attacked by fighters from rival factions, or bombed by an aircraft operated remotely by a person thousands of miles away whose intended target is a bad guy in your neighborhood. You probably have a place you call home that, although everything in it may not be perfect, isn't a place you have to leave with only the belongings you can carry and cross a border into another country hoping that the people there will at least tolerate your presence, if not perhaps welcome you.

Maybe you're a person who worked your entire life to become the type of person who can pay someone else to make them a cup of coffee, or maybe you got lucky and were born into a situation in which paying for something like a cup of coffee isn't a big deal at all. Either way, you've arrived at this point, and here you are with your cup of coffee and it's a nice day and you have a few minutes. Yes, maybe things aren't perfect, maybe your car isn't running quite right or your boss isn't recognizing your potential at work or you feel like you could lose ten pounds or the roof of your house is leaking or you're wondering when it's finally going to be your turn to meet the man or woman of your dreams or finally feel fulfilled in your career aspirations or just have enough time to do all the things you want. But hey, for right now, you have this coffee and a few minutes to enjoy it, so just do that.

5. Lift your coffee to your lips and, carefully now, take a sip of it—it might be hot.

DEAR FOAM ROLLER:

I think . . .

Oh, foam roller, you thought I was just going to say "fuck you," didn't you? Well, hold on. It's a little more nuanced than that. I hope you have a couple minutes.

I think I'm starting to understand our relationship a little bit, and I don't want to exactly thank you, but I kind of want to thank you. Kind of imagine me smiling as I reach to high-five you then faking you out at the last second and giving you the finger while scowling, but then shrugging my shoulders and high-fiving you for real a second later. Yes, I realize that sounds a lot like a metaphor for a lot of people's dating experiences.

Anyway: Thanks, fucker. I like to do painful things like running, for such long periods of time that parts of me don't like to work that well, and in order to keep doing those painful things, I bought you at a sporting goods store. Although I wonder if you're available at places that supply other S&M products? Seems like it might be a good fit.

So, every night for a while now, you and I have been rolling around the kitchen floor together. Actually, I roll on you. You're stoic throughout, and I wince and whine and make funny breathing noises. I put my bodyweight on top of you and roll you up and down the side of my thigh, where I'm told something called an IT band exists—on of those body parts you don't even know is there until it decide ruin your week, kind of like an appendix, but for runners. A I have complaints about that thing too, the IT band, bu unimportant as long as you keep doing your job. Which is apparently to make me cry through a weird sort of massage.

Some people think "massage" and see a warm, friendly face, someone who cares about your well-being, who is trained to figure out what's ailing you and why, and then, through understanding but firm human touch, heals what's wrong and makes you feel better. You know, a massage therapist. You, foam roller, are not a massage therapist. You are a sort of surrogate for a massage therapist, but not a good one. You approximate a massage therapist the way a body pillow approximates a real person, or a d—you know what, I'm going to stop there.

Basically, I do not think of a massage therapist when I think of you. I think of Gunnery Sgt. Hartman from *Full Metal Jacket* screaming, "You will not like me. I am hard, but I am fair." The more pain you cause, the more good I assume you are doing for my running/ultrashuffling career. Keep in mind I haven't had any professional training on how to use you, save for what a couple of friends have told me, and the videos from the folks at The Run Experience—who have introduced me to "East-West" rolling, which in terms of pain is like taking the leap from smoking ditch weed to smoking crack. Holy shit.

Has anyone ever used you for interrogation? Just a thought. There's this spot that I think is where my IT band and quadriceps meet, about halfway between my hip and knee, that I think could get me to give up classified information I was sworn to keep secret even upon threat of death, if it was foam-rolled just so.

Look, I guess I'm cool with what you do. I realize it's your job, and it's kind of my job to let you do your job. There are other things in my house that I think do much more joyous jobs, like the blender, the French press, and the ice scream scoop; but I guess not everyone has a super-fun, sunshine-and-rainbows gig in life, right? And you don't, so I shouldn't hold it against you. I think my IT band is feeling a little better this week, after our third or fourth session that consisted of you getting rolled over by me, and me squishing my face into several different configurations and making up new curse-word-strings for three to four minutes. And I guess that means we're doing OK, I suppose.

So I guess I should say keep up the good work.

shole.

F*&# BUSY

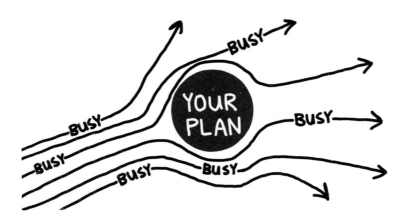

Alastair Humphreys, writer and adventurer on both macro and micro levels wrote a book called *Grand Adventures* a few years ago. Thanks to a shipping misprint, I ended up with two copies in my mailbox. So I put a post on Instagram the other night asking people to make a case for why I should send them the extra copy.

I wrote: "Who out there has a big trip dreamed up but needs a kick in the ass to make it a reality?" because I think Al's book is intended to do just that.

I didn't intend the Instagram post to be a case study, but after reading all the messages, I realized a lot of us need a quote-unquote kick in the ass, because, while we have a lot of great ideas or half-formed notions of adventure, we also somehow don't make time for them. So they stay dreams.

And when we say "dreams," there are two kinds: (1) the ones you have when you're asleep, in which you spend four hours trying to get a malfunctioning gas pump to work at a Shell station in the desert while completely naked except for a pair of oven mitts and a Pittsburgh Steelers helmet and for some reason your old college roommate's ex-girlfriend is there too, and (2) the kind of dreams that you think up on your own while you're sitting in traffic or staring out th window of your office for a few minutes and think about what you might do if you were somewhere else.

I am not a behavioral psychologist, but I think there are a number of reasons big trips/adventures don't happen in our lives. The biggest one is that we procrastinate about them, as if instead of being the coolest thing we might ever do in our lives, they are something like cleaning the gutters of our house or going to the dentist. Why do we procrastinate about big trips? We're busy.

Well, seriously, fuck busy. We're all busy now. Here's how it happened: a long time ago, you weren't busy. Then you got busy with a bunch of shit, some of it that you made up, and now you're always busy. That time long ago when you weren't busy, that would have been the time to take that big trip to South America or Scandinavia or Alaska, wouldn't it? You didn't have shit to do. Except you didn't have any money. Now maybe you have money, but you have no time.

Here's how you plan a big trip and make it happen: Look at your calendar. Yeah, I know it's busy—we already covered that. There is a point where you have nothing scheduled. Could be six months from now, could be eight months from now, could be a year from now. Keep the calendar open.

Now make a quick list of all the stuff you want to do in the magical time we call "someday." Some of the stuff is big, some of the stuff is small. Focus on the big stuff. The trips you'd have to take two or three weeks off work, or a month, or hell, just quit your job to do. Oh, but heavens no, you couldn't ever do that—yes you could. Pick one of those big things and figure out how long you would have to be away to do it. Two weeks? Great. Write it on the calendar, in the appropriate season (i.e., you don't want to try to do a weeklong backpacking trip in the Grand Canyon in July).

Now, do not break that date for anything. Find a partner for this adventure, someone who does not drift into "Flake Mode"—ever. Commit. Tell your boss about it and confirm that you will not be in the office those days. Treat this adventure plan as if it is a wedding. Weddings are bulletproof, because everyone knows how much planning goes into them. Even when shit completely melts down at the office, no one messes with the person getting married. Ever heard someone say, "Denise, I know you're getting married on Saturday, but we really need you to come in to the office . . . " Hell no, you don't. This adventure is your wedding. You are getting married to your dream, not procrastinating about your dreams any longer. Congratulations.

In the months between now and the time of your big adventure, you will still be busy. Guess what, busy is not going away for most of us. It's the new reality. Again, fuck busy. Work within it. The adventure you have planned is a giant rock in the middle of a river, and the waters of "busy" will flow around it. You are not going to magically find yourself "not busy" eight months from now. Your boss isn't going to stop piling shit on your plate. You are not going to "get caught up" and have a big sigh of relief and look at your calendar and go, "Would you look at that, nothing going on next week. Guess I'll just buy some tickets tonight and finally go to Bali tomorrow."

So make a plan now. That nagging feeling you have that your life is passing you by will go away, and be replaced by a very real need to buy gear and maps and to train and to talk a friend into going with you, as well as a joyous feeling called anticipation, which is about a million times cooler than procrastination.

HOW TO PACK
FOR A BIG TRIP

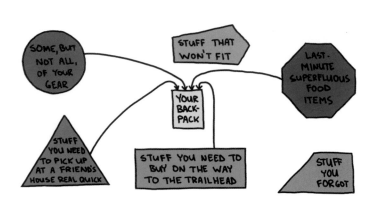

You just can't beat getting out of the office for a few days or a couple weeks to go skiing, backpacking, climbing, or mountain biking. But aren't you tired of sweating the details, checking and re-checking, having all your stuff together when it's time to go, and then knowing where everything is right when you need it? Boring, right? Here's how you can change all that:

WAIT UNTIL THE LAST MINUTE.

There's nothing like getting to bed early the night before a big trip and falling asleep knowing you've taken care of absolutely everything, and all you need to do is wait for your friend to pick you up, or get to the airport on time. Nothing like it *except* the adrenaline rush of having absolutely nothing done and running around like a madman or madwoman trying to find all your stuff. Instead, wait until the night before you leave, if not the morning of the day. If you're packing the night before, procrastinate even more by going to happy hour after work and knocking back one to five beers before you head home to start packing. If you have a nagging feeling that you "really should get going," remember, packing is not fun; beer is fun. Do more beer and less packing.

DON'T WORRY ABOUT FOOD.

Another cool thing to do last-minute is remember that oh, yeah, you might need some food for the trip. Head to the grocery store at 11 p.m. and just grab a bunch of random stuff that may or may not meet the various qualifications you'd usually have for adventure food, such as good taste, relatively light weight, and easy preparation. Better yet, pack little or no food, and don't tell anyone until you're out in the wilderness somewhere, preferably dinnertime. When everyone else is starting to cook, say something like, "So, could I eat some of your guys' food? I was going to bring some, but I just ran out of time."

PUT UNRELATED ITEMS TOGETHER.

A common strategy is to keep things that have similar uses together in the same stuff sack, or area of a backpack. Like bike tools, or toiletries. This makes it easier to remember and is similar to the organization you have at home: you keep your toothbrush in the same room you keep your razor and shampoo, and you keep your hammer in a box with all your wrenches and screwdrivers. That's great; but for some novelty, how about putting your toothbrush in with your backpacking stove, or keeping the rag you clean your bike chain with in your cooking pot? That way, every morning, you don't have to spend all that mental energy trying to remember where things go—just throw all your shit in your pack together. Got an expensive camera? Toss it in with your trash from last night's meal, and maybe some used toilet paper—or better yet, just put it all the way at the bottom of your pack, and then when you want to take a photo, ask all your friends to stop and wait for you to empty out your entire pack to get your camera from the bottom.

SEPARATE YOUR STUFF AT HOME SO IT'S HARDER TO FIND LATER.

Yes, when you bought your tent at the gear shop, it came in a handy stuff sack that held all the parts you needed to set it up. But what fun is that when it's time to pack? Instead, try to separate the poles from the tent and tent fly and the tent stakes, so when you're up at 2 a.m. the night before you leave, you have to locate four things, not just that one big bag. Extra credit for separating all your tent stakes and putting them in separate places—then you also have to try to remember how many tent stakes you actually need, i.e., "Let's see, that's one, two, three, four, five stakes, but I'm pretty sure I need more than that for the tent. Hmm, one for each corner, one for each door, yeah, six. Where is number six? Plus maybe one or two for guylines." This can go on all night.

KEEP SOME GEAR OFFSITE.

Nothing's better than when your friend comes to pick you up for Your Big Super-Fun Trip and you hop in the car and say, "Hey, we just have to run over to my friend's house across town and get my [backpacking stove, bike helmet, climbing shoes] real quick." This is especially fun if you're headed to the airport and you haven't factored in any leeway for delays like driving all over town to pick up your stuff. And even more fun if you hit a ton of traffic on the way to the airport.

DON'T ACTUALLY "PACK" UNTIL YOU'RE AT THE TRAILHEAD.

Yes, it would save a lot of time if your stuff was already in the proper backpack. When you and your friend(s) arrived at the trailhead, you could just hop out of the car and start walking, riding, or skiing, with minimal delay. But that would be efficient. Here's what you do instead: Carry all your stuff in a couple shopping bags or a duffel bag, and bring your backpack empty. When you get to the trailhead, start packing. This is the ultimate realization of waiting until the last minute (see "Wait until the last minute" above), and your friends will really appreciate it.

LEAVE SOMETHING ESSENTIAL AT HOME.

"Hey, before we get too far out of town, could we stop at a store so I can buy some sunglasses? I just realized I left home without my sunglasses. And sunscreen. And tent. And food." Another good move is to forget something really important and discover it when it's way too late to go back. Like saying, "Oh, shit, I forgot my tent poles" after you've hiked in 6 miles to a campsite (to forget tent poles easily, see "Separate your stuff at home so it's harder to find later" above), or saying "You are not going to believe this" to announce you forgot the rope the moment you arrive at the base of an alpine climb after a three hour approach hike that got you and your buddies out of bed at 1:30 a.m.

PACK TOO MUCH.

If you've done everything properly, you should not be zipping your bag shut any earlier than about forty-five seconds before you have to walk out the door to meet your friends or leave for the airport. Ideally, at this point, you cannot zip your bag because you've loaded it up with way too much shit, and you can enjoy the adrenaline surge of unpacking, reevaluating, and repacking all your stuff, all while hyperventilating because you're going to be late. If it does all magically fit in your bag while you're on your way to the airport, hopefully it weighs 55 to 75 pounds and you can experience the joy of unpacking, reevaluating, and repacking all your stuff at the airline ticket counter to avoid paying a fee for an overweight bag.

Have a great trip!

LOVE WHAT YOU DO, EVEN IF YOU DON'T "DO WHAT YOU LOVE"

REGULAR JOB

- SOME GOOD STUFF
- SOME BULLSHIT

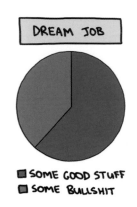

DREAM JOB

- SOME GOOD STUFF
- SOME BULLSHIT

I was sitting at a coffee shop with my girlfriend one day when she saw a sign hanging on the wall over my shoulder: "Love What You Do."

"That's interesting," Hilary said. "You always see it the other way around, like, 'Do What You Love.'"

As in, "Do what you love and you'll never work a day in your life."

I am one of those people who does what they love, in theory. I get paid to write, and sometimes make films, and sometimes stand in front of a room of people and run my mouth. I would be lying if I said it wasn't great, because after a decade and a half of job titles like dishwasher, busboy, waiter, bartender, custodian, assembly line worker, nonprofit development coordinator, reporter, editor, and retail sales associate, it feels great. But I would also be lying if I said my job wasn't "work," because it's only great sometimes. A lot of it, like everyone else's job, including yours, is bullshit I'd love to not have to do. Are you reading this at work? Just kidding. Of course you're reading this at work.

In a talk I gave at a college last year, I said that anyone who says, "Do what you love and you'll never work a day in your life," is full of shit, because everyone hates at least some part of their job. If it was 100 percent fun, it would not be called "work," or "your job"—it would be called "Sex" or "Eating a Whole Goddamn Pint of Ben & Jerry's by Yourself." I told those college students, if you love 30 percent of what you do and can tolerate the other 70 percent, you have won. (I did not say the sex/Ben & Jerry's line in the speech, for the record.)

Do What You Love is good advice to help people find what they initially want to do, but not everyone is looking for The Ultimate Fulfillment in a job, and not everyone is going to get a job that looks good on Instagram. I'm not being negative here, but we're not all going to grow up to be pro snowboarders, famous actors, or adventure photographers, or anyone else we think is "living the dream." Ninety-nine percent of the working population has a "real job," and no one should feel self-conscious about that.

The trick for most of the world is not necessarily Doing What You Love, but learning to Love What You Do, whatever that is. Obviously if you truly, deeply hate your job, you should quit your job; but if you're not going to quit, your job is a near- to long-term reality that you'll have to face forty hours a week or more.

There are people who can make any job miserable. There's a chance—and I'm not pointing fingers—that if every single day at your job, you think, "my job sucks," maybe you suck. The real trick is to find some sense of happiness in your work, whether it's mopping floors or managing a whole staff.

We've all met that bus driver or custodian or grocery store clerk who, after we walked away from them, made us think that they would be a great TV show host or stand-up comedian. And we wonder why they're not doing just that and sharing their personality with more people. But maybe they've got it figured out in being who they are for whatever audience they get, interacting with hundreds of people on a personal level every year, and just being happy adding joy to a job where making people smile isn't a requirement, but something extra they do in addition to driving the bus or ringing up groceries.

For a long time, when my mother would tell me to "have fun," I would say, "I am fun, Mom." Perhaps that's a good idea to keep in mind: Be fun. Yes, we're all at work. As previously stated, it is not all fun. But it doesn't have to suck. You're very likely going to work for at least forty years of your life, which is a hell of a long time to be throwing a pity party for yourself if you're that miserable person at the next cubicle.

There's honor in following your dreams in order to do what you love, but there's also honor in doing your job. Because maybe doing what you love is raising a family, rock climbing on weekends, learning woodworking skills after you leave your job every evening, or like my friend Ben, making money enough that you can donate an inordinate amount of it to nonprofit organizations. Plenty of artists, poets, writers, and filmmakers pull espresso shots to pay their rent. Brian Panowich, author of *Bull Mountain*, one of Amazon's top twenty books of 2015, is a firefighter in the state of Georgia—not *was* a firefighter—he still is a firefighter.

A few years ago, my Uncle Dan said he thought not every kid who graduated from college was going to be able to work in finance, and that you could make $40,000 a year driving a backhoe, which is a pretty good living—so why weren't we telling more kids to do that? Is it "doing what you love"? Well, I know a lot of little kids—and adults too—who would light up at the thought of sitting inside a big yellow piece of construction equipment. More than once in the past six months I've wondered how great it would be to start my work day by climbing into the cockpit of one of the 100-foot-tall cranes I see in downtown Denver, instead of flipping open a laptop. Is that crane operator living the dream? I don't know, not very many people can tell you what it's like to build a skyscraper. Seems pretty cool to me.

We're all special, and we're all not that special, too. We're not so far removed from the last recession to forget that by having a job, you're living the dream, too. Almost nobody's getting out of bed in the morning going, "Yay, work!" But we should be saying, "Yay, life!" And work is part of that, whether you clock in to pilot an airplane, a shovel, or a spreadsheet.

ON "FEAR DISGUISED AS PRACTICALITY"

> • I'M TOO BUSY • I'M TOO OLD FOR THAT SHIT • I'M
> AFRAID OF IT • I'VE NEVER BEEN GOOD AT THAT
> SORT OF THING • I WASN'T RAISED THAT WAY •
> WHERE I COME FROM WE DON'T DO THAT • I
> HAVE A MORTGAGE • I HAVE A BAD BACK/ BAD
> KNEES/ BAD HIP • I DON'T SPEAK THE LANGUAGE
> THERE • THERE'S NO WAY MY BOSS WOULD LET
> ME TAKE THAT MUCH TIME OFF WORK • I'M
> TOO COMFORTABLE WITH THIS LIST OF PERSONAL
> LIMITATIONS I'VE GROWN TO KNOW AND LOVE

On all the stops on one of my recent book tours, I showed a slide that's a list of reasons people don't do things: bad knees, mortgage, not enough vacation time, too old, et cetera. They're things I've heard people say, or I've said myself at times, usually following a phrase like "I would love to do that, but . . ." or "I wish I could do _____, but . . ."

I don't want to give away too much, but one of the themes of my book *Sixty Meters to Anywhere* is realizing the difference between a) a real reason we can or can't do something and b) bullshit. Or figuring out that many of the stories we tell ourselves could, if we're honest with ourselves, be translated into the same three words: "because I'm scared."

Everyone has a list of things they theoretically would like to do: raft through the Grand Canyon, do a weeklong motorcycle tour in Vietnam, start a blog.

And everyone has a list of "practical" reasons they can't do all those things, too: I can't take that much time off work. I don't know how to ride a motorcycle. Writing a blog is a waste of time unless a ton of people read it and I can make money off it.

There are solutions to all those reasons you list: Ask your boss about something called "unpaid time off" (or just quit your job). Take a class on how to ride a motorcycle and get your license. Sell some stuff you don't use or get a second part-time job for a few months.

There are no special people who are born with a magical ability to do bold things. There are, however, people who choose to look at challenges and find ways to do them, instead of talking themselves out of them. I have been lucky to meet dozens of these people in the outdoors and in creative work—people who are not sure if they can climb El Capitan or Denali, but try, or aren't sure if they can make a short film or start a photography business, but go for it anyway.

A couple weeks ago at a climbing gym in Iowa, I climbed with a seventy-one-year-old woman who started climbing indoors in her late sixties. Kitty climbs mostly with men in their twenties and thirties, because at her home gym, men in their twenties and thirties are most often available to belay. I watched her sail up a crimpy 5.10a/b route and a few others, and the only time she said the word "can't" was when she was explaining the extensive warmup routine she does before she climbs—"I can't just jump onto routes first thing like you young guys."

If anybody communicated to Kitty that Iowan women in their late sixties don't just take up rock climbing, she didn't listen. Maybe she's thought of a bunch of reasons she shouldn't be trying to redpoint 5.10 routes, but hasn't deemed any of them worthy enough to stop her from trying. Obviously the practical thing would be to take up something a bit more sedentary, like Sudoku or knitting—or to just say, "I've never climbed before, I'm in my late sixties, and I don't know any rock climbers, so I can't climb." But of course she didn't do that.

In his 2014 commencement speech at Maharishi University, actor Jim Carrey told graduates, "So many of us choose our path out of fear disguised as practicality." Meaning: We tell ourselves the right thing is the "responsible" thing, instead of the thing we dream of someday doing. We put a lot of effort into coming up with different reasons that sound better than saying "I can't do it because I'm scared of what might happen if I tried." It sounds practical, so we make ourselves comfortable with practical decisions.

Most people would never tell you that their dream in life is to be as practical and comfortable as possible, but we often end up striving for those things unconsciously. But no one writes an end-of-year holiday letter and brags, "Every time I thought of something really cool

I could do, I found a way to talk myself out of it so I could stay home instead: there was a marathon I didn't sign up for in March because I didn't think I had time to train, the family vacation we decided to put off for another year because we scheduled too many other activities over the summer, and the job I really hate going into every morning but stayed at for another year because I'm nervous about interviewing for a more challenging job."

Plenty of people on this planet don't have the privilege to choose between practical and impractical, but if you are fortunate enough to be in a position to dream of things that scare you a little bit, consider the real source of your anxiety about a big idea.

Obviously free-soloing *Moonlight Buttress* or trying to climb K2 solo in the winter is a different story when you have a family at home. But when it's something like "I'd love to hike the John Muir Trail/climb Mount Rainier/write a screenplay but I have too much other stuff going on this year/I'm redoing our basement/I'm not one of the people who does big bold things like that," you might ask: Am I really being practical, or am I just scared?

OUT OF OFFICE AUTOREPLY: I'M IN NATURE

Out of the Office July 10-14 Re: Your e-mail

Brendan <brendan@semi-rad.com>
to you ▾

Mon, July 10, 11:15 AM

Hello,

• I'm in nature somewhere
• My phone is off
• Sorry / not sorry

[Reply] [Forward]

Thanks for your email. I took the morning/afternoon/day off to ride my bike, or go rock climbing, or go for a jog in the park nearest to my home, or read a book while sitting next to a lake or stream, or something like that in nature, which is the stuff you see in between or outside of the urban areas where we live and work. It is often green and/or brown, or other such earth tones. I go there sometimes to, as someone once put it, "take my soul to the laundromat." I inhale, I exhale, I let my shoulders down a little bit, and relax my facial muscles, especially my forehead, which I realize I tend to crinkle too much when I'm anxious about something.

I will not be responding to your email until I return from nature. I did not take my computer into nature because there is no Wi-Fi there, and I probably didn't take my phone with me either, and if I did, it's in Airplane Mode, or as I call it, "This Phone Is Now Only a Camera and Music Player" mode.

In addition to not answering your email for a few hours, here's some other stuff I will not be doing:

• Checking Facebook, Instagram, or Twitter for interactions with other human beings in hopes to verify in some small way that I still exist and/or matter

- Checking Facebook, Instagram, or Twitter for things that might entertain me for two seconds to five minutes while I procrastinate about things on my to-do list
- Remembering that I have something called a to-do list
- Checking my email every five minutes so I don't have to focus on the work I should be doing
- Feeling my cortisol levels increase when my phone vibrates to alert me that someone on planet Earth has interacted with me on some platform or is trying to reach me via electronic means
- Communicating with anyone who is not speaking to me face-to-face
- All the other things that I typically deem important but I realize are kind of bullshit once I get outside my personal Bubble of Busy

I will get back to these things in a few hours, once I am finished with my Nature Time, which I believe is essential to physical and mental well-being. If, while awaiting my response to your email, you'd like to read about some studies that validate this belief, check out "This Is Your Brain on Nature" by Florence Williams, an article published by *National Geographic*. Or "How Walking in Nature Changes the Brain" by Gretchen Reynolds, an article published by the *New York Times*.

If you are contacting me for an urgent matter that you believe requires immediate attention, please take a deep breath and consider your definition of the word "urgent" and the phrase "requires immediate attention." Perhaps you, or you and Denise, or you and Dave, or whoever, can figure out a solution to this urgent matter before I return to email. In the event that you cannot devise a solution, perhaps you can do something else for a few hours and patiently await for my return to electronic communication.

In the event that waiting a few hours for an email response from me becomes too much to bear, I humbly suggest you locate the nearest park and walk there for a few minutes, leaving your phone at your desk and instead concentrating on looking at trees and birds and clouds.

Thank you,
Brendan Leonard
www.semi-rad.com

REVIEW: WATER BOTTLE

About twelve years ago, I bought a water bottle with no water in it. I guess it was kind of a thing in the outdoors world, a bottle that you could take with you so you didn't have to buy several bottles of Dasani or whatever every time you wanted to go on a hike. It worked out pretty well on the trail, so I just started taking it everywhere with me. I started to drink water often, because I heard that the human body works better if it has water in it. Seems to be working OK so far.

Since that first water bottle, I've gone through a few different bottles, some plastic, some stainless steel. The current one I have is blue, and silver in spots where the blue has chipped off over the past year and a half. It works pretty well for the one thing I ask of it: to hold water and not leak said water all over my other stuff. High-five, water bottle.

So let's break it down. What are some of the good things about this "reusable water bottle" concept?

1. IT SAVES MONEY.

That's right. I drink probably three liters of water a day. If I drank all that water in the form of bottled water, I'd spend $5 a day. Even if I halved my water consumption, I'd spend $2.50 a day, or $912.50 a year. Or if I bought my bottled water in bulk at Kmart, I'd spend $1.25 a day, or $456 a year. I mean, what kind of fucking aristocrat do you have to be to afford to drink bottled water? What's next, paying for bottled air to breathe? So I just fill up my water bottle using faucets and water spigots.

Yeah, I paid $29 for this bottle when I bought it, but at my highly-addicted rate of drinking water, I figure it's saved me $600 to $1,300 in the past year and a half. And I suppose I spent that money I saved on espresso or burritos, two things that take some actual skill to produce, unlike water, which flows over the surface of the earth and is apparently filtered and tested multiple times daily in US municipalities (big asterisk here for the jerks responsible for the current debacle in Flint, Michigan). And then a soda company bottles the water and sells it to you in a plastic bottle. Or: you stick it to the man and get your own reusable water bottle and fill it yourself while imaginary cash registers cha-ching in your head.

2. I DON'T HAVE TO DISPOSE OF IT EVERY TIME I EMPTY IT.

It's saved me from having to lug 1,000-plus plastic bottles to a recycling bin somewhere, or otherwise deal with them, over the span of a year. I mean, if you threw one plastic bottle into the corner of your living room every day, you'd have a mega-pile of them by the end of the year. Not to mention this visual reminder of your exorbitance. Or perhaps you're into that, and you'd use it to show off, like "Look what a rich son of a bitch I am—I just drink out of these containers once and toss them in the corner. That's right, I PAY for super-special bottled water. Every day." Anyway, I have a pretty small apartment, so it's not really an option.

3. CONVENIENCE.

Most reusable water bottles are sturdy, and way harder to spill than, say, a glass of water from your kitchen cupboard at home. You can put the cap on, twist it until it's tight, and then turn the bottle sideways, upside-down, whatever. Then it can roll around on the floor of your car, or hang out in a backpack with your laptop computer and you don't have to worry about the water leaking out everywhere. Not to talk shit about glasses, but really, their usage is pretty limited when it comes to travel. When's the last time you saw someone hauling ass through the airport to catch a flight with a glass of water in their hand? Yeah, that's what I mean. Yet with my water bottle, I recently did just that—and was able to stop and fill it up from a "water fountain," a source of free water that flows out of airport walls at the mere push of a button.

Overall, as far as water storage and delivery receptacles go, I give reusable water bottles a thumbs-up. From the bottom of the Grand Canyon to the top of the Grand Teton to every airport I've been through, and all the other places I don't want to lug a 26-pound 24-pack of bottled water, reusable water bottles have been there for me.

Five out of five stars. Would fill up with water and drink from again.

THE VALUE OF JUST GOING

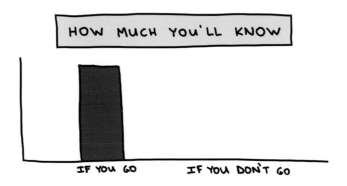

Last Saturday afternoon, I was about to nod off in the passenger seat of my friend Mitsu's car while we drove across Portland. I was exhausted, the kind of tired that comes from a week of consecutive nights of not enough sleep and too much to do. But Mitsu wanted to ski Mount Adams with our friend Kendall, and weeks ago I had agreed to join. I was so tired when we were packing Mitsu's Subaru that afternoon that I tossed my laptop in the back of the car just in case I decided to bail before we got started the next morning, and could at least get some work done. The stoke level, you could say, was almost imperceptible.

We went to bed at 11 p.m. I unzipped my sleeping bag at 3:20 a.m., wishing I had known what happened to the breakfast burrito I had bought the day before, for just this moment. Then I left my glacier glasses on the dashboard of the car as we started hiking at 4:05 a.m., skis and ski boots strapped to our packs. I walked at the back of our group of five, trying to keep words like "nap," "bail," "tired," and "donuts" out of my mind as the sun slowly rose in the east and the ghost-white silhouette of Mount Adams filled up the sky to the north.

I've been trying this trick lately, when I am semi-dreading what I know will be hard, or what the lazy person inside me doesn't really want to do: I talk myself into just starting it. When I tell myself I'm going to run four laps around the park near my house, I want to quit after one lap. So I just make myself start Lap No. 2. Then No. 3. Then No. 4. Pretty soon, at about the forty-five-minute mark, I hate running less and actually start having fun. And it's the same thing with a trail run, a climb, or whatever: I know I like these things, but I have buried that thing that makes you go, the thing that 100 percent knows that whatever it is will be fun.

I'm trying to be one of those people you might know, the people a lot of my friends are, who default to motion, who aren't happy unless they've moved in some way every day. But I default to eating emotionally, trying to check things off my to-do list, and being sedentary—all things that are satisfying sometimes, but usually less rewarding than the hike, or the climb, or the camping trip that you keep putting off and then, suddenly, it's October.

You just have to *go* sometimes. Ignore all the little voices in your head that can list a million things a minute that you need to do or would be more comfortable doing, and put on your damn running shoes, or pack your backpack, or get your gear out of the garage and throw it in the car. Maybe it's not perfectly planned, or you won't be able to get as far as you would like, but three miles is probably better than no miles, isn't it?

The person you want to be would go, and the person you want to take care of would take a nap or just keep clicking around the internet and scrolling through feeds, hoping something halfway interesting might pop up. If you choose to *not go* often enough, eventually you'll wonder where all the time went, and what you did with all those hours—because you won't have any photos or memories of them.

Almost eight hours after we started hiking up the trail to Mount Adams, with a stop to put skis and skins on, another stop to take them off and bootpack, a stop to put skis back on, and four breaks to eat breakfasts Nos. 2 through 5, we popped onto the summit of Mount Adams, 6,700 feet above the car, and with a bluebird-sky view of Mount St. Helens, Mount Hood, and Mount Rainier. I clicked into my skis and began the ski run of my life, down 4,000 vertical feet of soft spring snow in Adams' Southwest Chutes. And once again, I couldn't believe how hard it had been to talk myself into coming. That guy I was yesterday, who was "exhausted" and thought maybe he'd be better just taking a day off? What a fool.

WHAT SKI PASS ARE YOU GETTING THIS YEAR?

Hey, are you getting the Super Mega Mountain Ultimate Combo Pack Pass this year, or what? I know it's already September, but I haven't decided quite yet.

It's a tough call, as you probably know. I haven't decided between the Super Mega Mountain Ultimate Combo Pack Pass and the other one, the Ultra Total Peaks Super Multi Pass. I know, it seems like a no-brainer, with the Super Mega Pass giving you access to three resorts plus four days each at the other three resorts, plus 1.5 days each at six resorts in four states that are only a $250 flight away if you go on a Tuesday, for only $899. But I did that last year and I was unable to take advantage of those extra 1.5 days at the other six resorts in four states that don't border my home state.

Plus I just started seeing this person I met on Tinder and they're really into the Ultra Total Pass, which in contrast to the Super Mega Pass, is only $649, and gives you unlimited access to the three resorts slightly closer to where I live (less than two hours if you leave at 6 a.m. on Saturday and don't stop to pee on the way up there), plus three days at that other super-chill place that's only forty-five minutes away and is kind of cool for a few days of skiing but I would never buy a season pass there. Because if the dating gets any more serious, it's going to be super awkward if ski season starts and I have a Super Mega Pass and they have an Ultra Total Pass. I mean, how are we supposed to grow a relationship if we can't ski on the same mountains the whole season? We might as well just say goodbye on November 15 and pick it back up on April 1, because I'm sure as shit not paying full-price for lift tickets at those places. That's like $90 a day, plus parking.

My buddy says he has a friend who's like some sort of mathematician who went to MIT but dropped out, and he apparently designed an algorithm that will decide which ski pass is the most bang for your buck. I don't know how it works, but the guy says the Ultra Total Pass is the way to go. But there's no way the guy could factor in which has the best terrain, because—and I know this is personal preference—I really think after about four or five weekends of skiing at all three mountains covered under the Ultra Total Pass, I'm pretty much bored. There isn't enough tree skiing, except at that one place, and the other two mountains don't have enough steep stuff. But I think the traffic is worse if you're trying to ski weekends and you go to the Super Mega Pass mountains. Oh, you disagree? Yeah, it's kind of a tossup, isn't it.

Anyway, who knows if that MIT dropout guy doesn't work for one of the big ski corporations anyway? I mean who the hell designs these ski pass deals, right? It *has* to be some MIT mathematician, doesn't it? Shit is so complicated. It's almost as confusing as trying to decide which paper towels are the best for your money, or which health insurance plan to get.

So I'm leaning toward the Super Mega Pass, I think. Mostly because I have been reading long-range weather forecasts, and a higher fraction of the Super Mega Pass resorts are supposed to be hit more with storms coming from some sort of jet stream or La Nina/El Nino/La Abuelita pattern or something like that. But I have another date tonight with that person who has the Ultra Total Pass, so if it goes well, everything could change by tomorrow morning.

What are you going to do? Oh, you're selling all your shit and moving to Jackson or Telluride in October? Yeah, that's probably less confusing. Well, have fun. I gotta put some more work into these pros and cons of the Super Mega Mountain Ultimate Combo Pack Pass and Ultra Total Peaks Super Multi Pass lists before my date tonight. Maybe I'll see you out there this winter. Or not.

TEN BASIC RULES FOR ADVENTURE

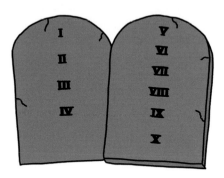

A couple years ago, my book *The Great Outdoors: A User's Guide* came out, representing about twelve years' worth of poking around in the out-of-doors—climbing, backpacking, hiking, skiing, trail running, mountain biking, bike touring, and just about everything else. I haven't climbed Everest, but I've survived a few hundred days of all those other activities, and a few hundred nights sleeping under the stars. And if memory serves, I think I'm still friends with 100 percent of the people I did those things with. So I put together a list of tips and ideas that I think will help you (1) stay alive and (2) not piss off your friends.

1. GET YOUR PRIORITIES IN ORDER

In any adventure, be it a five-mile hike or a multiday climb, this is my list of goals, in numerical order:

1. Don't die.
2. Have fun.
3. Get to the summit/campsite/lunch spot/waterfall/whatever.

Prior to his attempt on K2 in 1995, American climber Rob Slater famously told a climbing magazine, "Summit or die, either way I win." He summited, but died on the descent with five other climbers when weather conditions abruptly changed. To each his/her own, but if I were to adapt Slater's quote to reflect my own ideals, it would be something more like: "Summit or live another several years to eat deep-dish pizza, either way I win."

2. AVOID FAILING TO PLAN

If I learned one thing from my climbing mentor Lee, it was this: If we say we're meeting at 5 a.m., be there at 4:30 a.m. with all your stuff packed so we can start doing whatever it is we're supposed to be doing that day. Not: Show up at 4:45, spend fifteen minutes rooting around in my car trying to find all my gear, fill up water bottles, change shoes, take a dump for ten minutes, and then realize I don't have my headlamp.

I mean, do you like waiting? Me neither. That's why I always appreciate people who have their shit together, like Lee. And I strive to be one of those people.

Here's one addition to this point: I know I am very, very stupid in the early morning. So I pack the night before. I put all my stuff in my backpack, and I lean the backpack against my front door, because then there's no way I'll forget anything—the rope, my climbing shoes, the entire backpack (which I'm not saying has happened, but could). Being an idiot is one thing—figuring out how to prevent yourself from doing idiotic things is another. Signed: A guy who has definitely shown up for a day of climbing without the rope, and another day with mismatched shoes.

3. AVOID JUST HOPING SOMEONE WILL FIND YOU

If you don't know Aron Ralston's story, here's the short version: He went canyoneering by himself in 2003, got his arm trapped behind a boulder, spent 127 hours trying to figure out what to do, and then cut the arm off with a dull, knock-off multitool. Plenty of people who haven't survived 127 hours alone in a slot canyon with their arm trapped under a rock can tell you all the things Aron Ralston did or didn't do correctly, but Monday morning quarterbacking aside, I think we can all learn one thing from his survival story: Always tell at least one person where you're going and what to do if you don't come back on time.

Ralston likely survived that misadventure because of two things, one being he's enough of a badass to cut off his own arm, and two being that his mother hacked into his email account to try to figure out where he was after she hadn't heard from him for several days.

Nothing against my mom's computer skills, but I'm not counting on her to guess my password if I'm out stranded with a broken leg somewhere for a week. Instead, I tell someone where I'm going, when I plan to return to civilization, at which time I will text them that I'm OK, and who to call if I don't contact them. Pretty simple, and way easier than hanging out in a freezing slot canyon for five and a half days and then cutting off your own arm.

4. AVOID SPENDING THE NIGHT OUTSIDE FREEZING

I have a little stuff sack I throw in my backpack whenever I go anywhere, whether backpacking, hiking, climbing, skiing, whatever. It has a space blanket and a headlamp in it. The headlamp is so I can find my way back to the trailhead if it gets dark, and the space blanket is so I can survive a night outside if I can't get back to the trailhead. The headlamp weighs three ounces, and the space blanket weighs three ounces. That's a pretty good insurance policy for something that weighs about as much as two Clif Bars.

An Alaskan guide told me once that the best place to pack extra batteries for a headlamp is in a second headlamp, so if I'm on a multi-day trip, I often do that. If I'm only going out for one day, I figure my iPhone has a flashlight on it, so that will probably work if my headlamp dies.

5. AVOID GETTING LOST

In the olden days, just as I was starting to get into the mountains, you had to carry a paper map with you to know where you were going. Often times, you had to figure out where to get USGS quad maps, and order as many as four of them to cover the right terrain. Nowadays, like a lot of things, adventuring is much easier. Maps are online, and there are a billion tools you can use to get ahold of the correct one. I still love paper maps, because the battery never dies, the screen never cracks, and there's zero software that has to function correctly in order for them to work. Also, I don't need cell service to use one. So if I'm going on a trip somewhere unfamiliar, I get a map for that area and go over it before I leave.

In addition to that, I carry a lightweight compass (yes, your phone has one, but again, phones break/die/don't work correctly sometimes), which is handy for figuring out where to go and usually doesn't need to be super-fancy in order for you to orient your map correctly.

And: I take my phone with me. There are several GPS apps you can use for navigation, including Gaia GPS and ViewRanger, and those are very useful for off-trail navigation, or just turning on your phone to see where you are on a map in relation to the terrain—you're the little orange arrow on the north side of the lake, or little blue dot on the east side of the peak, or whatever. Note that most of the time you'll have to download the appropriate maps *before* heading into an area where you won't have cell service.

6. AVOID NOT BEING ABLE TO MACGYVER IT

We love to say duct tape fixes everything, which is almost true. Duct tape will usually not fix a flat on your mountain bike when you're six miles from the trailhead, for example. But it will work to prevent blisters from ruining your life, to temporarily patch a hole in your rain fly, or to hold the sole on your hiking boot for a few miles. Of course you should carry some other stuff too, depending on your sport/situation.

You don't need to haul a box of tools and a bunch of repair stuff everywhere you go, but a few things can save the day when your gear breaks down. I generally have a few items I swap in and out of a stuff sack that goes in my pack whenever I'm out a few miles from a trailhead. Including, but not limited to:

- Duct tape (obviously)
- Single-serving super glue tubes (great for skin cuts as well as other minor repairs)
- Zip ties (for bike cables)
- Ski straps
- Baling wire (minor repairs to tents, snowshoes, other stuff)
- Cord and safety pins
- Needle and thread (if you stay at a nice hotel, swipe the sewing kit from the toiletries)
- All-purpose patch kit for clothing/tents
- Multitool (doesn't have to be mega-fancy; I rarely find myself opening wine or sawing tree branches with a multitool in the backcountry, but your needs may be a little different)

7. AVOID LIGHTNING

This one may seem pretty obvious, but I bet anyone who's spent a significant amount of time in the mountains can tell you at least one story about a time they were way too close to a thunderstorm (myself included). You don't have to be a meteorologist to figure this one out: Small clouds are OK, but when clouds start to build and get taller, a storm could be brewing. Basically in Colorado every summer day, it's going to thunderstorm in the afternoon sometime.

What should you do? Get somewhere where you're not the tallest thing. i.e., don't be on top of a mountain, or on the side of a mountain above tree line. Get to lower altitude, in tree cover. If you can't get there and a storm comes in, your last resort is to get far away from anything metal you're carrying, drop your backpack, stand on your backpack (so your feet aren't in contact with the ground), and then crouch down and hug your knees. You probably won't feel safe, but it's the best you can do—that's why it's called a "last resort."

8. AVOID CRITTER ENCOUNTERS

Unless you're a tourist driving around Yellowstone, you probably recognize that animals that weigh more than three hundred pounds are dangerous and not something you should approach as if they are Minnie Mouse at Disney World. This is a good policy. In addition to having physical implements and skills that can slash or smash you to death, pretty much every piece of megafauna in the mountains can run way faster than Usain Bolt, so the safest distance to be when viewing a bear, elk, moose, bison, or other large animal is about the length of one American football field.

Don't feed squirrels, don't try to get a closer look at a mountain goat or bighorn sheep, and if you see a rattlesnake in the trail, get the fuck away from it. Forty percent of rattlesnake bites happen to people who have a blood alcohol content of 0.10 percent or higher (surprise), and forty percent of rattlesnake bites happen to people who are handling the snake at the time of the bite (no shit). If you're in an area where rattlesnakes are active, be aware, and don't haul ass down overgrown trails without taking a look under the brush at the edges of the trail (use trekking poles).

Also be aware of how much an animal getting into your food can ruin your day. Squirrels in popular climbing and hiking areas can unzip zippers and chew through backpacks and wrappers, and when they do, they'll probably eat bites of all your food before leaving. Keep them out of your stuff with screw-top plastic containers, which, although bulky, keep your PB&J free of hantavirus.

9. AVOID ENDING FRIENDSHIPS OUT THERE

If you communicate expectations, have your shit reasonably together, and in general don't create drama amongst your peer group, you'll probably be OK with this and your friendships will survive. Sometimes people have different goals (see previously mentioned "summit or die" quote vs. my "summit or live" idea), and this can produce friction. If you can avoid being a jerk to your friends and adventure partners for the duration of your hike/trip, you can stay friends. If your friend doesn't have that laser focus on finishing the climb or staying out all day skiing in nasty weather, don't sacrifice the friendship for some contrived adventure goal. One day, you might find yourself thinking, "I really wish someone would go to the new Wes Anderson movie with me, but I was such a dick to Jeff/Jen when we were skiing, I can't ask him/her now."

10. DON'T BE AFRAID TO BAIL

If you always summit, always finish the climb, always have a great day out skiing, and never get shut down, well, please call me, because you apparently have the best luck ever. The fact is, if you spend enough time trying to do things in the outdoors, you're going to fail sometimes. You will have to sit in a tent for a day or two in a rainstorm instead of finishing the big loop backpack you wanted to do, you'll have to rappel off three pitches shy of the top, you'll have to abandon a day of skiing because of bad avalanche conditions. Sometimes it's OK to realize that going would suck way more than not going. One time a few years ago, my friend Mitsu and I arrived at the Lumpy Ridge parking lot for a day of climbing and found ourselves getting pushed around by 35-mph wind gusts. I said I thought the route we were doing was still probably OK, although the rappel might be a pain in the ass in the wind. Mitsu said, "I'm not worried about it being dangerous. I'm worried about it being not fun." And we drove into town and got coffee instead, which was both fun and not dangerous.

TWELVE WAYS TO HELP THE WORLD FEEL LESS HOPELESS

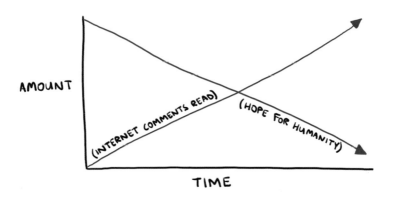

1. Don't argue with people on the internet.
2. Use your car horn to communicate with other drivers for emergencies, not to communicate your frustration with other things in life.
3. Pretty much 100 percent of the time, people don't want to be surprised by photos of male genitals.
4. Try to be the first to yield the trail when you see a hiker or mountain biker coming.
5. Clean the bathroom. Doesn't have to be your bathroom, doesn't have to be a complete cleaning. Maybe just pick up a paper towel and throw it in the trash can, even if it's not yours.
6. If you don't have any money for the person with the "anything helps" sign, just ask them if they're doing all right.
7. Read a book that has a perspective of years or decades, instead of more tweets and status updates reacting to the last few minutes or hours.
8. Let someone onto the freeway.
9. No matter what, don't read the comments section.

10. If national news gets you down, do something that helps locally.
11. Instead of insulting someone over their opinion, ask a few questions to try to understand how they came to form that opinion.
12. Instead of talking on your phone while talking to a server/barista/bartender/customer service representative, ask the server/barista/bartender/customer service representative how they're doing. Actually, in general, if you treat people like people instead of like robots doing tasks or soulless internet avatars, you might find you have way more common ground than you assumed; and even if you don't, you might discover that that person, although having different opinions than you on many subjects, is still a pretty decent human being who, like you, likes beer and/or likes bicycles and/or likes baseball and/or likes Star Wars and/or has kids they're really proud of and/or has a parent or grandparent dying of cancer and deep down, probably doesn't ever want bad things to happen to people, but, you know, the world is a complicated place. And maybe if we all tried listening instead of picking teams and bickering, we might be able to fix some shit.

TWENTY ALEX HONNOLD FACTS

HALF DOME LEANS ON ALEX HONNOLD

Perhaps you have read about Alex Honnold's groundbreaking ropeless climb of El Capitan on June 3, 2017. Here are a few things you may not have known about Alex Honnold, many of which are also quite impressive.

1. Alex Honnold did the Rim-to-Rim-to-Rim in the Grand Canyon in two big steps.
2. Alex Honnold hand-jammed the entire Monster Off-Width on *Freerider*.
3. Alex Honnold has paddled a whitewater kayak from the summit of Mount Everest to Base Camp, in winter.
4. Alex Honnold correctly predicted 100 percent of his NCAA Tournament bracket in last year's office pool.
5. Alex Honnold eats nine servings of fruits and vegetables per day.
6. Alex Honnold understood *Ulysses* the first time he read it.

7. Alex Honnold has never had a problem connecting to the Wi-Fi network anywhere.
8. Alex Honnold got the new Jay-Z album two weeks before it came out.
9. Alex Honnold onsighted your project.
10. Alex Honnold's van is zero-emission because it runs on the world's collective awe at his climbing achievements.
11. Alex Honnold set an FKT running the John Muir Trail barefoot while only eating plants he found along the trail. And he high-fived a black bear.
12. Alex Honnold used all his vacation days last year.
13. Alex Honnold surfed Teahupoo on the back of a tiger shark.
14. Your dog is normally quite skittish around new people, but took immediately to Alex Honnold.
15. Alex Honnold is secretly the creator of many of your favorite memes.
16. Alex Honnold completed an Ironman Triathlon riding a razor scooter for the bike segment.
17. Alex Honnold's old climbing shoes smell like lilacs.
18. Alex Honnold is actually also Jimmy Chin, and photographed himself free soloing *Freerider*.
19. Alex Honnold parallel parked his van in a very tight space yesterday without even slightly bumping the cars in front of and behind him.
20. Your cousin's friend met Alex Honnold at an event a couple years ago and Alex Honnold was very friendly to him.

FIFTY-TWO PIECES OF ADVENTURE ADVICE

Everybody has a few one-liners that always crop up in their head when they're out hiking, skiing, climbing, and/or having a good time or bad time outside. I brainstormed a few bits of this advice I've remembered over the years from mentors, friends, authors, plus some of my own mantras, and a few that Facebook friends sent me. Hope some of these save your ass, or at least put a smile on your face.

1. Always bring a headlamp.
2. The best place to keep extra batteries for your headlamp is in another headlamp. (An Alaskan guide whose name I've forgotten)
3. When you feel low, eat and eat more. When you feel good, slow down. (Vivian Doorn, advice about 100-mile races)
4. Don't buy gear, buy plane tickets. (Yvon Chouinard)
5. Don't try to muscle through anything—just keep spinning. (My friend Mick, on long-distance bike touring)
6. Always carry a spoon. You never want to miss out on free food.
7. Always take a big bowl or mug on a group trip, or go hungry.
8. Ounces equal pounds, and pounds equal pain. (Unknown)

9. Don't get in your sleeping bag with damp socks on.
10. Don't expect a great night of sleep while camping—expect a series of naps.
11. When you wake up wondering if you should get out of your sleeping bag/tent to pee or if you can get back to sleep without getting up to pee . . . just get up and go pee.
12. Check your knot. (Chris Kalous)
13. A helmet almost always protects your brain more than a stylish hat.
14. Pain is just a feeling. (Steve Swenson)
15. Geologic time includes now. (Gerry Roach)
16. Sometimes eating's not about liking. (Jayson Sime)
17. Always make sure the cap is on your water bottle.
18. If it hurts to walk and it hurts to run, running will hurt for less time. (Brody Leven)
19. Commit. (Meghan Hicks, on ultrarunning)
20. If you can follow it, you can lead it.
21. Sunburns are for amateurs.
22. Basically you just don't want to fall when leading ice climbs. (Lee Smith)
23. It's not really a "dry suit." It's more like a "slowly getting damp suit." (David Marx)
24. Eventually, they all become rock skis.
25. Don't say, "photos don't do it justice." Somebody's photos do.
26. Somebody can ride that on a hardtail.
27. Only do one stupid thing at a time. (Shannon Walton)
28. Start cold.
29. The more you know, the less you need. (Yvon Chouinard)
30. If you're going to go ultra-light, make sure you have ultra-experience. (Nicole Dautel)
31. The odds on very difficult climbs are not in your favor. So there's no excuse to show up unprepared, to show up out of shape. (Kelly Cordes)
32. When skiing in the trees, don't look at the trees, look at the spaces in between.
33. There are no bad adventures, just bad company. (Libby VandeKamp Littler)
34. That's the thing about goals, they don't just fuckin' lie down for you. (Jayson Sime)

35. There's really no such thing as a self-arrest once you get going on a steep slope—you really have to stick the landing if you fall. (Lee Smith)
36. Never stand when you can sit. Never sit when you can lie down. (The first rule of mountaineering)
37. Going one mile an hour with zero breaks is faster than going two miles an hour and stopping to catch your breath every five minutes.
38. Most tents are no good without the poles.
39. Don't plan on it not raining.
40. There are two easy ways to die in the desert—thirst and drowning. (Craig Childs)
41. Learn how to fix a flat tire and always carry a spare tube.
42. Breathe.
43. It's easier to stay out than get out. (Mark Twain)
44. You'll be fine. (Alex Honnold/anyone who's ever sandbagged a friend)
45. Pick your partners first, then the objective. (Penn Newhard)
46. Ideal circumstances rarely make for interesting stories. (Scott Nowacki)
47. If you wouldn't ski it WITHOUT your avy beacon, you still shouldn't ski it WITH your avy beacon. (Peter Wadsworth)
48. If you always eat your best food first, you'll always be eating your best food. (Unknown NOLS instructor)
49. Never judge the weather from your sleeping bag. (Phil Powers)
50. Go average, go often. (Reid Pitman)
51. If there is a solution to the problem, why worry? If there is no solution, why worry? (Bill Thompson)
52. Wear a hat. (My mom)

BEARS DON'T CARE ABOUT YOUR PROBLEMS

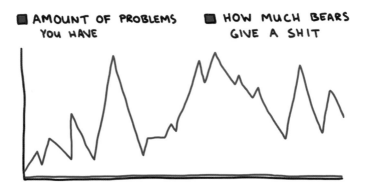

AMOUNT OF PROBLEMS YOU HAVE　　**HOW MUCH BEARS GIVE A SHIT**

Bears don't care about your problems. Call your mom, tell your Twitter followers, or take a Sharpie and write them on the wall of a public restroom if you must, but bears certainly don't give a shit.

Bears do not care how many likes your bikini selfie got on Instagram today. Bears do not care if the grocery store was out of your favorite almond milk. Even if you have slight anxiety because you haven't mowed your lawn in a while and it's more than ankle-high, bears could not care less.

Did you drop your phone and crack the screen? I know, AGAIN? Don't go looking for a bear to commiserate with you. Bears don't have phones, or sympathy for humans who can't take care of nice things like the $700 computers we keep in our pockets, or set on the table while having lunch with a friend because we now have the attention span of a goldfish.

Bears do not care if you are not feeling motivated, or if you aren't happy at your job, or if you are just SO BUSY all the time now. Bears are busy too—busy spending zero time wondering how you're doing out there in the non-wilderness parts of the world, and instead focusing on their own survival, which is a little less trivial than the stuff you've been complaining about. Like you, bears have not been putting much money in their 401(k). But bears don't have 401(k)s, or any sort of money system. Or retirement.

Bears don't want to hear about your new diet, what you're avoiding eating, or what you're only eating now, or how it makes you feel, or not feel. You can eat rocks and die, for all bears care. Bears are eating everything they goddamn can right now, and by the way, don't you think they're looking a bit more athletic compared to last summer?

Just kidding. When it comes to fucks bears give about what you think, the official total is zero.

Bears are not arguing about politics with their uncles at awkward family get-togethers, on Facebook, or anywhere. Bears are not sitting in a Starbucks with their friend Christy telling her about what that toxic bitch Kim said to Jen about them last week, even though they hate drama and the only reason they're telling Christy is because she doesn't see Kim for who she is. Bears don't worry about gossip.

Bears can run 30 miles per hour, though, which is faster than Usain Bolt, for the record.

Bears are out there, doing their shit, being "in the moment" like we all talk about wishing we did a better job of. Bears are not meditating and trying to find their center. They are trying to find food, keeping track of their kids, and occasionally destroying other species that fuck with them. Then they sleep. Bears do not have time for your shit.

Bears are, however, very interested in the food you bring into their habitat, and do not have very good manners, or really any perception of property rights. So, if you're backpacking or camping in bear country this summer, make sure you use a bear canister or properly hang your food from a tree before you go to sleep at night.

BIRTHDAYS (AND OTHER DAYS) SHOULD BE MORE LIKE FUNERALS

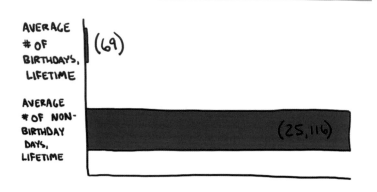

I went to a memorial for the son of some friends recently. He was a climber and a skier, and died in his late twenties, far too soon by almost anyone's definition of life. The memorial was wonderful, with hundreds of friends and family members attending, and more than a dozen speakers of varying relations throughout his short but impactful life: teachers, fellow students, climbing partners, mentors, friends. It was the kind of thing you'd hope your friends and family would do for you when you finally go, if you were to make as big of a mark on as many people as he did.

When we lose someone, we tell stories, we reminisce, we laugh, we cry, and we try to figure out how to come together and properly deal with the new void in our lives. It's a deeply meaningful illustration of the saying "You don't know what you've got till it's gone." We say things we should have said to that person the last time we saw them or talked to them on the phone, we talk about all the things we loved about them to the other people in their lives who can appreciate it, and we generally come together in a big group hug that's missing the person in the middle of the whole thing.

You probably only get a few parties in your life, and only a couple of those are very well-attended by everyone you consider important: your wedding and your funeral. The wedding is for you and your spouse, and the funeral is for everyone else. Depending on your metaphysical view of the universe, you may or may not be in attendance at your own funeral in some form. Whether you can or can't hear the great things people say about you once you're gone, if you're honest, you'd have to admit that most of us are probably appreciated more at our own funerals than we are in real life.

I've been a Scrooge about my own birthday for a long time, saying things to my girlfriend like, "Who cares? All I did was stay alive another year." Instead, can we celebrate this book that took me ten years to get published, or a film project I lost hours of sleep over—but another birthday? I cringe whenever people sing "Happy Birthday" to me, and cringe for anyone who bears the (in my opinion) misfortune of having it sung to them in a crowded restaurant. Why not actually say the wonderful/meaningful things we'd say at someone's funeral on their birthday, when we're ostensibly celebrating them? Or, just the next time we see them?

At the memorial last weekend, I thought of how great it would be to hear all the stories, memories, and tributes like the ones shared at your funeral—but while you were still alive. How much happier we all would have been if the event was a birthday party instead of a memorial. Of course that's impossible—but couldn't most of us do a better job of expressing gratitude for people while they're still here? I mean, the Happy Birthday song is fun, but it doesn't say much of anything. I don't mean birthdays should be morbid, or ignored, but maybe they should be a little more thoughtful.

Telling someone "happy birthday" is one thing. Saying "I love you" is obviously much better. But how often do we actually put some effort into saying something specific and authentic? Thanks for visiting me in the hospital. I admire your ability to always say the right thing. I'm grateful that you share your perspective on life with me.

In the past couple years, I've started to realize that I have quite a few friends who send cards to each other. Not clever birthday cards with funny messages in them, but generic cards with a few sentences handwritten on the inside: Thanks for being _____. I appreciate your _____. Glad you're in my life.

Near the end of last year, I bought a couple dozen cards and took a few hours to send them to friends, because I wanted to be one of those people who sent heartfelt, handwritten cards. It ended up being an exercise in gratitude (on my end), and appreciation (hopefully felt by the person who received the card). I suck at remembering friends' birthdays, but I was able to make time over the span of a couple days to remember why those friends were important to me and write them a quick note. And I don't remember that many birthday gifts I've received over the years, but I have much clearer memories of those notes of appreciation that came straight from friends.

Funeral rituals have been around for as long as humans have, and they're of course important for all of us in processing death. We have 365 days of each year of someone's life, birthday or not, to communicate our gratitude to them, and currently dozens of avenues to do that. There's absolutely nothing wrong with the way we celebrate someone's life after it's over, but maybe we should all consider finding more ways to celebrate them while they're still here.

BUT DID YOU REALLY CLIMB IT?

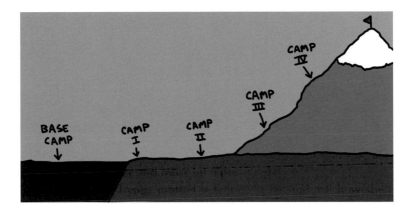

Near the top of the Palmer Snowfield on Mount Hood, the two mountaineers had been skinning uphill for about 2,600 feet when they saw the end of the snowcat track at about the 8,500-foot level.

"Wow, the snowcat goes up this high?" the first mountaineer said, slightly out of breath.

"It appears so," the second mountaineer said, also breathing hard. "It used to take climbers up this high to start their ascent of the Hogsback Route."

"But that's almost halfway!" the first mountaineer said.

"I know!" the second mountaineer said. "Are you even climbing the mountain at that point?"

They shuffled their skis a few feet higher on the hard snow, hoping the sun would soften it before they started their descent.

"However," the second mountaineer said, "You and I did drive to the parking lot, which is much higher than your house back in Portland. Almost 5,800 feet higher, in fact."

"Indeed," the second mountaineer said. "Perhaps we should have bicycled from my driveway for a more pure ascent?"

"Or walked," the first mountaineer said.

"Walked from the ocean, actually," the second mountaineer said. "That would be the purest form of alpinism."

"Yes, I think so," the second mountaineer said. "Except we also should have done this without crampons, ice axes, and skis. Those are artificial climbing aids."

"You're correct," the first mountaineer said. "We should have done this climb with nothing but alpenstocks, in order to claim a pure ascent."

"What the fuck is an alpenstock?" the second mountaineer said.

"You know, those big tall sticks they used to climb Mont Blanc in the 1700s," the first mountaineer said.

"Ah, yes," the second mountaineer said. "But I think no alpenstocks, because they are artificial and would taint a pure ascent of the mountain."

"OK, no alpenstocks," the first mountaineer said. "And probably no high-tech clothing then?"

"Exactly," the second mountaineer said. "No high-tech clothing. Actually, no clothing. We must climb the mountain naked. Boots are artificial coverings for the feet."

"Also," the first mountaineer said, "Since the only true climb of a mountain is the first one, we must find mountains with no established routes to their summits, and then climb only those mountains."

"Yes," the second mountaineer said. "Beginning with our feet in the ocean. Completely naked. And we will eat no food other than what we can gather and hunt on our way to the mountain."

The men were silent for a few minutes.

"Climbing things is kind of ridiculous," the first mountaineer said.

The men skied higher, removed their skis, put crampons on their boots, climbed to the summit, skied down, and then drove to a diner to drink milkshakes.

DEAR NEW GUY AT THE CLIMBING GYM

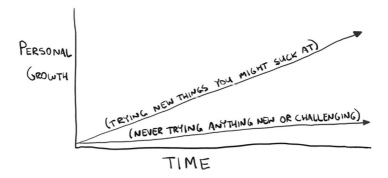

Dear New Guy at the Climbing Gym—or lady running around the track at the park for the first time, or person trying out hiking, mountain biking, or skiing, or lifting weights, or whatever for the first time:

Good for you. Yes, good for you for just trying something new. Maybe you're wondering if you're doing it right, or if you have the right clothes or technique, or if you don't exactly blend in. All of that stuff is OK.

Sure, maybe a few of the people you see doing the same thing look more comfortable doing it, or you think they're way better than you'll ever be. Well, they probably are more comfortable. But when they look around the gym, or the trail, or the mountain, they see someone who they think is way better than they'll ever be. And even if they're the best climber or skier or runner in the immediate vicinity, they are no doubt aware that someone else out there is better than they are. Everyone's trying to get better at whatever it is they're doing, no matter how long they've been doing it.

We're all beginners once, and only once. The nice thing about starting out—versus already having done this for years—is that you're going to get better in big leaps and way faster. You'll become stronger and more confident, lose more weight, or whatever it is you're trying to do, at a much faster pace at the beginning. Don't forget that, because it won't always be that way. Your progress will become increasingly incremental, and sometimes feel invisible, the longer you do it. So enjoy being new at this.

Do you feel like people are looking at you, maybe judging you because you're not doing it right or you look like a newbie? They're probably not. And if they are, they're doing it to deal with their own insecurities, which is of course not exactly the adult thing to do here.

So just keep trying, don't be afraid to ask for some help or advice, and you won't regret it. It's way better to try something new and worry that you suck at it than to never try that something new because you were worried you might suck at it. Closing yourself off to new things out of fear eliminates the chance to be brave, whether you're scared of heights, scared of crashing in the middle of a ski run, or just afraid to look bad in front of other people a few time as you learn.

Not everyone will ever be "the best," but everybody can try hard. See you out there somewhere.

Signed,
A Guy Who's Slightly Less New at This Thing And
Just Wants Everyone to Have a Good Time

FIND A WAY AROUND—
OR THROUGH

A few years ago I was at a coffee shop and I started chatting with the guy next to me about what I do for a living, which, at that time, was barely getting by trying to be a full-time outdoor writer after recently quitting my last full-time job. The guy said he was interested in photography and would love to somehow do some adventure photography someday.

I said, "That's great, I have a few friends and acquaintances who are photographers and lots of them have similar stories on how they got started: get outside with friends, shoot a ton of photos, and figure out a way to sell them."

He said, "Yeah, but it's hard because magazines are hard to get into and I don't know anyone at any companies and _____ and _____ . . ."

I said, "Sure, yeah, it's definitely hard to get your foot in the door at first, but maybe it's something you pursue part-time for a while and see where it goes and then eventually it could grow to full-time. That's what I did."

And he said, "Yeah, but This Reason I Can't Do It and That Reason I Can't Do It."

I decided I better get to working on whatever was on my laptop screen instead of talking to the guy, because I wasn't going to be able to talk him out of any or all the reasons he couldn't do something he theoretically wanted to do someday.

I used to collect rejection letters from magazines, book publishers, and literary agencies. This was back when you used to write letters to people first to pitch them your idea for a magazine article or book. I got them from *Outside, Backpacker, Sierra,* and dozens of literary agents and publishers, with all pretty much the same message: three or four sentences saying "thanks, but no thanks, and good luck."

The first rejections really crushed me—I was young and naive, and had poured my heart into crafting pitches that I was sure that particular magazine or publisher would love. But they didn't. And they really didn't seem to care how their rejections made me feel (although I'm not exactly sure how they would have communicated that—maybe sending an intern in person to deliver a hug and an encouraging pat on the back?).

One spring, when I was putting together photos for a slideshow for one of my book tours, I found a file of rejection letters, probably forty of them. Which was not even close to all of the rejection letters I received back when people used to write letters. I laughed, then laid them all out on the floor and took a photo of them.

Fortunately for me, the publishing industry is full of stories about bestselling books that were rejected more than one hundred times (*Zen and the Art of Motorcycle Maintenance,* for one), so I just figured that was all part of it. I kept writing and reading adventure stories and books, and noticed they all had one thing in common: Nobody ever wrote, "And then it got really hard, so we quit."

Everybody has an idea or twenty, of things we'd love to do, if only. If only we had a little more money, or a little more spare time, or a little more space in the garage. We could do that trip, climb that mountain, start that business, write that book, make that film. We get that thing done, or we don't get it done. Whether the reasons are valid or just lame excuses, the thing gets done or it doesn't.

People want to see you do the thing that makes you come alive. Nobody wants to listen to you complain and list all the reasons why you can't do it. (Probably a few people in your life will listen, but not for that long.) Whether it's running an ultramarathon or learning to play the guitar, if you want to do something enough, you'll find a way around all those reasons, or through them. If you don't want to do it enough, you can have a seat at the bar with all the other people who would have done something great: if only. Pick a cliche: life is hard, life isn't fair, nobody owes you anything. I'll tell you what, it's easy to sit and drink beer and talk about doing shit. It's hard to do shit. But it's good for everyone.

FLAKE ON ME ONCE . . . ACTUALLY, JUST DON'T FLAKE

A couple weeks ago, a friend shared on Facebook an opinion piece by David Brooks titled "The Golden Age of Bailing." The first comment was someone saying it was futile to try to find a reliable climbing partner in the town where they lived, and a second person chimed in and said it was impossible in the town where they lived a few hundred miles away.

David Brooks is not the first person to point out that we're devolving into a culture that's more and more accepting of bailing or flaking on plans we've made. People point at technology, or the fact that we have so many options of things to do, or the fact that we're all "so busy" nowadays that it's easy to double-book yourself. But here's the root cause of flaking: You do it because you're inconsiderate, which is bullshit.

Call me old-fashioned, but when my friends say, "I'll be there at 10 a.m. on Saturday to help you move that couch," they show up, and that fucking couch gets moved. And I value that. Especially when it's something more important than moving a couch—like showing up on time for an alpine start for a day in the mountains and being there with an avalanche beacon with full batteries, or keeping me on belay from the second you say "on belay" to the second you say "off belay."

I don't know how the Fitz Traverse began, but I'm pretty sure it didn't start with Tommy Caldwell waking up on the first day of their weather window and sending Alex Honnold a text message saying, "Dude, sorry to bail on you, but I'm tired from this week. I think I'm just going to stay in and watch *House of Cards*." Big things get done because people show up to do them, not because they half-ass some plans, kind of commit, show up late, and get lucky.

We live in a society where we get pissed and demand to be compensated if our flight is delayed, or if the food we ordered at a restaurant takes longer than acceptable, because we're offended that someone is not doing their job correctly. And then we make an appointment to meet someone and show up twenty-five minutes late—or not at all. We treat our friends like we think airlines treat us, and somehow that's OK.

Yes, things come up, and sometimes they're important things. Your kid fell off the monkey bars and you have to take her to the hospital to get stitches, so you're going to miss coffee. Your boss called an emergency staff meeting at 4:30 and if you don't go to it you probably won't be on the staff anymore, so you're going to have to reschedule your happy hour meeting. But everyone knows the difference between a reason and a bullshit excuse. Being late because of traffic not under your control is one thing, but being late because you scrolled through twenty more Instagram photos before you left for your promised meet-up is another thing, and it sure as shit isn't being "busy."

If you want to get shit done, it's very simple: show up. Do what you say you're going to do. And demand from yourself the same accountability that you expect from an airline. Your partners for climbing, skiing, biking, and moving furniture will appreciate it.

HONEST CLIMBING GYM PARTNER WANTED ADS

I WANT TO GIVE YOU BETA

You: A decent climber. Me: An expert on every route in this gym, even the ones the route setters are halfway finished putting up as I write this note. I know all the route setters—Dave, Serena, Jason, Carly, and Alex—and I know their climbing styles, what they like and don't like, and how they communicate their likes and dislikes with the routes they put up in this gym. Want to know everything? Climb with me and I'll tell you the minutiae of every single move of every single route here, even the 5.7s. Don't want to know anything? I'll tell you anyway. While you're climbing the route. I will tell you exactly where to put your feet, how many pads you can get on that hold, and when you're doing all of it wrong—because chances are, you are doing it wrong. I climb here Mondays, Tuesdays, and Thursdays, from 4 p.m. to 10 p.m.

LET'S CUT THE SHIT, I'M JUST LOOKING FOR SOMEONE TO MAKE OUT WITH

Man looking for a partner for Tuesday/Thursday evenings from 6 p.m. to 8 p.m. I lead 5.11c–d but am not picky about how hard you climb as long as you can give a good belay. And in the event you are a single woman who reads this and doesn't really like climbing and just wants to get a drink, I would love to do that too. If there's mutual attraction, I am willing to completely give up climbing and do whatever it is you like to do on Tuesday and Thursday evenings. Let's talk.

I SEEK ATTENTION

If you climb here, you've probably seen me working my project—or, rather, heard me screaming at the upper section of one of the techy, overhanging routes here in moments of extreme effort and then frustration. I sometimes sulk and/or pout when I just can't get the final crux sequence. I am not "psyched" on climbing so much as I am adversarial. I do not enjoy it; rather, I approach it as a bullfighter approaches a bull—it is to be danced with, then killed. Except, unlike a bullfighter, I never wear a shirt and I make lots of grunting noises and the occasional shriek. If you find the noises a cat makes when it gets into a to-the-death fight with another cat inspiring rather than terrifying, email me at the address below and we can climb together on Tuesdays and Thursdays.

BOULDERING MAKES ME SAD AND LONELY

I come here by myself and I climb for two minutes and then rest for five minutes, looking at all the problems in the bouldering area until it's time to climb again. I repeat this ten to fifteen times and then I leave. I just want to get higher than 15 feet off the ground. Please belay me and I'll belay you and we can be friends. Or not be friends, whatever works for you.

I PROMISE TO KEEP 80 PERCENT OF MY ATTENTION ON OTHER PEOPLE AT THE CLIMBING GYM, 20 PERCENT ON BELAYING YOU

Partner wanted for mostly 5.10 to 5.11 routes where, when it's your turn to climb, I can talk to other people or just keep my head on a nearly-360-degree swivel to see if anyone is looking at me, is interested in talking to me, or is an attractive person who might be interested in me. Don't worry about it, I got you.

JUST WANT SOMEONE TO TALK AT

Are you a good listener? Have you ever dropped someone while belaying? If the answers to those two questions are "yes" and "no," respectively, let's climb! I am here Mondays, Wednesdays, and Thursdays from 5:30 p.m. to 8 p.m. and I have a lot of things I need to express. I'm not looking for conversation, I just want to talk. As long as you nod your head every once in a while and acknowledge both my existence and that there are words coming out of my mouth, I'm sold. I climb mostly 5.10s.

I AM OSTENSIBLY LOOKING FOR A CONSISTENT PARTNER TO KEEP ME MOTIVATED

I have big climbing dreams and goals and believe I just need the right partner to hold me accountable by committing to a regular training schedule. Want to climb here three evenings a week and keep each other psyched? Me too, hypothetically. I'll show up all three agreed-upon days of the first week and climb hard with you, and maybe even all three days the next week too. But then something will come up and I'll miss a day the next week, and then another day the next week, or maybe two. Then I will stop letting you know when I am or am not coming, and you'll show up and just climb with other people instead of waiting around for me. Don't take it personally—it's not you, it's me. How do Mondays, Wednesdays, and Thursdays work for you?

I BELIEVE IN INERTIA

"YOU GOT A PIANO TIED TO
YOUR ASS OR SOMETHING?"

– MY MOM

It happened again yesterday, like it always does, about three-quarters of the way through my run: I tried talking myself out of finishing. My stomach was acting up, I could tell I was dehydrated, I was sluggish from not getting enough sleep the night before. What's the difference, really, I asked myself, between 4.5 miles and 6 miles? Who would care, really, if I went home early?

But I didn't. Because when this happens—and it happens inside my head all the time—I have a trick I use. I make myself start the last lap. I've run probably a thousand laps around the 1.45-mile crushed-rock trail around the park near my house, and I wouldn't say I've enjoyed many of them. Almost every lap is a small battle for me, but I've figured out one thing: if I can get through 10 percent of a lap, I'll get through 100 percent.

I have plenty of friends who are happier in motion than they are at rest, and I have realized I am not one of them (although my mother is). I could sit and eat donuts in front of a computer screen for sixteen hours a day and it wouldn't bother me a bit, so I've had to devise systems to keep me from giving in to my sloth-like instincts. I refuse to own a reclining easy chair because I've seen them trap people for hours. I commit to outdoor events beyond my capabilities so I'll be terrified enough to train for them.

I believe in inertia—large or small, physical or psychological, it's a wonderful and horrible thing. A body at rest will stay at rest, sometimes for years, and a person in a job they don't like will stay in that job long past when they should have quit. We stick with routines that are bad for us simply because those routines are comfortable. It's called inertia.

In trying to figure out both sides of that equation, I've learned something about myself: If I take that first step, I'll commit to the rest. I've stood nervous at the top of steep ski runs, at the bottom of ice climbs or rock routes, and backstage before public speaking gigs, and the worst part is the few seconds or minutes right before you say fuck it, you stop worrying, and you go. You make the first jump turn, swing one of your tools into the ice, edge the rubber of your rock shoe onto the first hold and step up onto it, or walk on stage and say the first few words. And then you're in it. Good or bad, falling or sending, at least you're not wasting mental energy worrying about it anymore.

Whether you want to run six miles or thirty miles, you have to run ten feet first.

I GAVE UP COFFEE
FOR THREE MONTHS
AND THIS IS WHAT
I LEARNED

If you talk to people about drinking coffee, they will often say things like "I just love the ritual of making coffee" or "I just love the taste."

I gave up coffee for three months this summer, and I'll tell you the truth: I'm in it for the drugs. The caffeine. The good shit.

Yes, the taste is nice and I enjoy the ritual too. But I drank some decaf coffee this summer, and the taste of decaf and the ritual of making decaf, and the *decaf* of the decaf, didn't really do shit for me. I just got sad for the first couple weeks I wasn't drinking real coffee, and then learned to live without it for awhile because I was giving it up for something more important.

Lots of people can't or won't do caffeine for a lot of reasons—no disrespect to that. But I've been drinking coffee for two decades and I can probably count the days I've gone without coffee on two hands. So I thought I'd share how my summer without coffee went.

Here's why I did it: I was training for an ultramarathon for six months, and I have experienced pretty bad dehydration problems (that have also, I am fairly sure, led to altitude sickness at various times) because of my coffee habit (which is, admittedly, probably a bit excessive). So starting June 8, I stopped drinking coffee.

In the days leading up to June 8, I stepped down my consumption to avoid caffeine withdrawal headaches. I still got the other withdrawal symptoms, like a slight depression (not making this up) that lasted for two weeks.

I joked to a friend that quitting coffee was going OK, aside from the feeling that life was meaningless. I was only partly joking.

I've experienced quitting a number of things. I quit drinking in March of 2002 and haven't had a sip of alcohol since, quit eating meat in September 2005, and quit smoking (from a pack-a-day habit) in November 2005. All were difficult to give up. I still miss pepperoni pizza and getting bombed on good beer ("I just love the taste!"), and for the first six months of not smoking, I missed the pleasure of standing outside, staring at nothing and thinking, for five minutes twenty times a day. And I may be forgetting some of the discomforts caused by all three of those things (the way you do with mountaineering and hard backpacking trips), but coffee was equally shitty to give up.

I hate ordering decaf in coffee shops, probably worse than I do turning down offers of beer and wine at restaurants, raft trips, baseball games, happy hour functions (OK, everywhere). I missed being able to give myself a little bump of 150 to 200 milligrams of caffeine during long travel days, early morning alpine starts, and drowsy afternoons at my laptop.

But here's the big thing I learned: I don't "have to have coffee." I just really like it. Probably the same with all the substances we imbibe.

Some things I did with zero coffee:
- Functioned for nearly twenty hours on just three hours of sleep the previous night
- Stayed awake for forty-two hours (while in constant human-powered motion for thirty-six)
- Drove a car for more than eight hours straight
- Got out of bed at 1 a.m. to climb mountains and actually summitted
- Stayed up until 2 a.m. editing video

- Continued to write and create for a living
- Still had insomnia induced by anxiety (dammit)
- Ate three ounces of dark chocolate (an entire bar) almost every day, which gave me somewhere between 30 and 100 milligrams of caffeine every day

The things that didn't happen:
- I didn't have nearly as many problems with dehydration while doing twenty- to thirty-mile trail runs in 80- to 85-degree heat.
- I did not have as many headaches.
- I didn't visit a fraction of the coffee shops I usually do (which is a primary means of socializing when you work from home as a writer).
- My dentist found nothing worrisome—for the first time in years—during my routine checkup (this could also be attributed to my using an electric toothbrush, but it's worth noting).
- I did not die.
- I did not become an asshole.
- I was not unbearable to live with, according to my girlfriend.
- I did not lose friends who love coffee.

I also found that when I was on long trail runs, the 50 milligrams of caffeine in a half package of Dark Cherry Clif Bloks felt like a rocket booster, since my body was no longer accustomed to high doses of caffeine (When you're drinking 400–600 milligrams of caffeine per day, 50 milligrams feels like a drop in the bucket.)

Quitting for three months felt like a major marker had been taken out of my day. Lots of people mark the end of a work day with a beer, I marked the beginning of a day with coffee: "I will drink this brown stuff, and be productive immediately after." I gave up that punctuation mark for three months, and just learned to live without it every day. I forced myself to wake up, to work, and to exercise without the jolt of caffeine.

To be honest, it really wasn't that difficult. I think I've learned over the years that we can often quite easily live without the things we think we can't live without (including but not limited to substances like coffee, alcohol, and nicotine). It might be good for you to try it yourself.

Me, I'm done quitting coffee for now. I love a good Americano from a skilled barista, I love shitty diner coffee, I love drinking coffee out of mugs of all shapes and sizes, I love sitting in coffee shops and working with the background din of good music and people having conversations. I love the ritual, and I love the taste.

But let's be honest here: I'm mostly in it for the drugs.

I HATE RUNNING

I hate running, three to four times a week if I have time. I hated it yesterday for a little over an hour.

I have three different pairs of shoes I hate running in. Every time I run, I pick one pair, and I go out and run in them, and I enjoy it about as much as I enjoy brushing my teeth in the morning—except running lasts way longer.

I hate running until I run for fifty minutes. There is some magical thing that happens right around the fifty-minute mark, where I start feeling like smiling at people I see or petting their dogs, and I absent-mindedly forget that I am not having fun.

Running is tiring. A couple times last year I did it for eleven hours straight, and man, was I tired afterward. Most days I do it for about eleven minutes before I'm like Fuck This. But I just keep going.

Sometimes I do some math in my head and think about being faster, and how much less time I'd have to spend doing this if I could run, say, six-minute miles instead of nine-and-a-half-minute miles. Then I think about something else, like how the outside of my ankle hurts. And I keep running.

Nowadays lots of people are excited about Fitbits and other fitness tracking devices, trying to get to 5,000 steps every day as a sort of baseline goal for fitness. I wasn't one of those people until my friend Dan showed me the "Fitness" app on my iPhone and told me there was no way to shut it off. Then I realized what a lazy piece of shit I am every day—except on the days I run, when I dominate that 5,000-step count thing by three or four times.

All the shirts I wear running smell like B.O. I wash them, and when I head out for a run, I put on a clean shirt, and it smells nice for a few minutes. After approximately forty strides, something in the armpits awakens, and they smell exactly like they did at the end of my last run. It's like I didn't even wash the shirt.

I also hate when, while running, I get about two or three miles from my apartment or the nearest trailhead, and I experience what I call "The Drop." The Drop is that rumbly belly pain indicating something is a bit amiss in your digestive system and it's giving you a warning shot, that you have probably a fifty-fifty chance at getting home or somewhere else private before you need to sit on a toilet. Although the idea that it's fifty-fifty is misleading, because while some of the time it goes away without further event, sometimes the end of the story is more thrilling than the first chase scene in *Mad Max: Fury Road*, and sometimes you end up squatting behind a bush somewhere. Anyway, The Drop basically only happens while running. You never get halfway up a route at a climbing gym and have something like that happen.

My friend Syd hates running, too. He's run in a bunch of New York City Marathons and other races, which he occasionally claims to enjoy. I asked him one time how much of his years-long running career he'd enjoyed, and he said, "You mean like total hours and minutes?" I said yes. "About fifteen minutes," Syd said. Which sounded about right to me.

Maybe the sickest thing about the whole idea of running is when you sign up for an organized run, like an ultramarathon, and in order to run 50 or 62 or 100 miles in one day, you basically have to spend about six months running all the time just so you can run that far in one day. You get to the finish line of a 50-mile race and people are like, "Congratulations, you just ran 50 miles." And you're like, "Fuck that, I just ran 750 miles—you just saw the last 50. Anyway, let's go get a pizza." And then you hate yourself and make strange noises every time you stand up from a seated position for about five days and then you start thinking, "That race was so fun, I should do that again soon." Sometimes I like to say, "I've done dumber things for worse reasons."

I also like to say, "I'm not sure that I like running, but I like having run." Which is kind of a joke, but not really. I mean, have you ever just let yourself mouth-vacuum deep-dish pizza and not stop until you were ashamed? Yes. Way more fun than running 31 miles.

So there's that, the calorie replacement, and a handful of other things about running that are likable. Chocolate Clif Shots, for instance. Sometimes I think about filling up a Camelbak reservoir with Hershey's Chocolate Syrup and going for a long run, and how awesome that would be, but the cleanup would be a pain in the ass, so I'm glad someone has thought of my needs and carefully packaged chocolate energy goo in small foil packets so I can hate my life decisions a little less approximately every thirty to forty-five minutes while running.

Also, there's a sort of meditative quality in the rhythm of it, when you do it for long enough. You can't make a good action sports film about it because it's not sexy like hucking cliffs is, but there's something to plodding along at a ten-minute-mile pace for hours at a time, and getting to a point where you just stop thinking altogether. Around Mile 10 or 12, I often think how fucked up it is that this is what I have to do to get away from the three-minute circuit of checking my email, then Instagram, then Twitter, then whatever, then my email again, then finally going back to that thing I'm supposed to be working on. Someone has no doubt done some research on why this is satisfying—I haven't, but I can tell you it's vaguely enjoyable. Here we are, literally running away from our damn phones in the year 2019.

Some people hate running so much that they don't run at all. They stay in shape riding bicycles, or doing circuit workouts, or using other machines at the gym. I'm not quite in that category, although I was for a decade or so. I guess I'm now in a category of people who hate running, but not enough to stop doing it. I imagine some people have the same feeling about prescription painkillers or day trading.

Maybe running is that pop song you know you absolutely hate, but if it comes on the radio when you're in the car by yourself, maybe you'll listen to the whole thing without changing the station. Or it's that super-cute guy or girl you just can't stand, but if they asked you out on a date, you'd drop everything and go out with them. Or maybe that's too philosophical, and running is just better than getting soft.

So I'll be over here, lacing up my shoes, wondering how my running clothes can smell so bad when I just washed them, procrastinating my run until the last possible minute, not really understanding why, just doing it, thinking of Denzel Washington in *Fences* yelling at his son, "Like you? What law is there sayin' I got to like you?" and wishing it was over before I even start, the whole time with a deeply buried subconscious awareness that there will probably come a day when I can't run anymore and I'll miss the hell out of it.

Anyway, I hate running. But you should totally try it.

I PLEDGE ALLEGIANCE TO THE GRIND

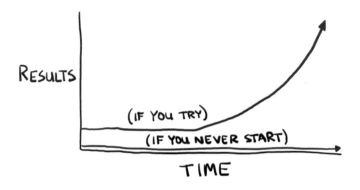

"A lot of the young doctors I hire work for me for a year or so and then they want to get out and do their own thing," my friend Tony Breitbach said a few months back. "They say, 'I want what you have.'"

Meaning they want a successful business of their own, not to work for someone else. Tony is a chiropractor and entrepreneur in Chicago. He sets his own schedule, goes on a few vacations every year, has some nice things, and has fun the majority of the time he's awake. Of course young doctors want what he has.

"I tell them, you're seeing me after ten years of work," Tony said. "You're not seeing me at the beginning, when I had literally zero patients, and I was out knocking on doors to get my name out there. I gave free seminars in Whole Foods and two people would show up."

Tony is telling a story about work. I like his story, because he doesn't say he's successful because he's smarter than everyone else, or a preternaturally gifted chiropractor, or that he's figured out some secret. He says it sucked at the beginning, and he worked hard until something started happening. This is the grind.

Tony and I have been friends since high school, when we washed dishes together in a restaurant in the small Iowa town where we lived.

It was a pretty simple job, as most dishwashing jobs are: You washed the dishes as they come in. When you had washed all the dishes, you got to clock out and go home. It was a grind. Thirteen years after that, Tony and I bicycled across America, from California to Florida, in forty-nine days. That was, more hours than not, a grind as well.

I often get messages from people asking some version of the question, "How did you start doing what you do?" I assume they are asking how I became a writer (and not how do I manage to be in my late thirties and still not own a decent car). Maybe they want permission to get started, or maybe they want some sort of shortcut or secret.

Here's the secret: I sucked. I tried to tell stories for a long time, and most of them were not good (I'm sure plenty of people would say I still suck). Eventually, I sucked less, and one day, I exhibited enough non-suckiness to get my stuff published in a few magazines. Voila.

This may not be every creative's secret to "success" (whatever your definition), but that's mine. I imagine my friend Tony would tell you he has a very similar formula for success, because I know this is how he works: He studies things, he works to get better, he tries new things, he fails at some, he succeeds at some. And in the beginning of his career, he didn't sit back and wait for business to come to him, or make excuses. He swallowed his pride and walked around the neighborhood, knocking on doors.

Here's a quote from retired Navy SEAL Jocko Willink: "Don't count on motivation. Count on discipline."

Here's another one from MC/author/producer Blueprint, from his *Super Duty Tough Work* podcast: "Artists think that everything has to be free-spirited, improvised, organic—all these corny words that equal 'I'm lazy, I'm not gonna do shit.' They gotta be quote-unquote inspired—fuck all that. Dude, write down what you're gonna do and set a plan."

Lots of things in life can be a grind: your job, all the menial tasks you have to do to keep your small business running, your training to get in shape for some event you signed up for, the workouts you have to do to keep your ass or belly from getting too fat, the homework assignments you have to do to get your degree. Here's a secret: You can choose to believe in the grind.

That's how you climb mountains: you grind. That's how you write a book. How you learn to play the guitar. How you get better at anything.

You don't just nod off daydreaming and accidentally wake up on top of a mountain, or stumble over the finish line of a 50-mile race because you were bored on Saturday and thought you'd give it a try.

If you spend enough time humbly knocking on doors to get new clients, or trying to play guitar chords, or studying how to get better at something, or dragging yourself out of bed to train for something, maybe one day you'll meet some definition of success. And maybe you'll also understand that the grind wasn't just something you did to eventually get somewhere—but that the grind itself, and how you improved as a person during that time, was the important part.

LESS SERIOUS ACCIDENTS IN NORTH AMERICAN MOUNTAINEERING 2017

Every year, the American Alpine Club publishes *Accidents in North American Mountaineering*, a compilation of notable climbing accident reports from the previous year. Flipping through the book helps climbers recognize how climbing accidents happen, the common mistakes that can turn serious, and how to be safer in the mountains overall.

But every year, there are accidents that don't make the pages of *Accidents in North American Mountaineering*. The following are examples of those types of accidents.*

BRAND-NEW NO. 1 CAMALOT DROPPED
Colorado, Flatirons, Third Flatiron

On August 7, two climbers were on the Standard East Face Route with a set of new cams. The climber leading the fifth pitch, while trying to remove a 0.5 Camalot from his harness, accidentally unclipped a No. 1 Camalot from the same gear loop, and watched over his left shoulder as the No. 1 bounced 500 feet down the east face to the bottom of the formation, somehow not hitting any of the other parties and free soloists climbing the route below. The climber slowly looked over his right shoulder to his belayer (who owned the rack), shrugged his shoulders, and mouthed "sorry." The party finished the climb and rappeled without incident and searched the bottom of the east face of the formation for the dropped Camalot without success.

Analysis: Climbers on busy routes should always exercise care to not drop gear. Also, if anybody wants a brand-new No. 1 Camalot with a few dings in it, go poke around at the base of the Third Flatiron.

SNACKS UNSATISFYING
Colorado, Rocky Mountain National Park, Petit Grepon

On July 22, a female climber (31 years old) and her partner finished the eight-pitch South Face route and stopped on the summit to coil their rope and eat lunch. The female climber dug through her small backpack to find she had only packed an expired apricot-flavored energy bar and half a bag of seasoned cashews left over from the previous weekend. Hungry from the approach and climb, the climber chose to finally open the energy bar and grudgingly munch on it while watching her partner enjoy a turkey, Swiss, and avocado sandwich he had made that morning, which, although somewhat hard to keep together because of the slipperiness of the avocado, looked delicious. The climbers rappeled and finished the descent without incident.

Analysis: This disappointing lunch could have been prevented by proper planning. The climbers planned the climb two weeks in advance of the date, and the female climber had plenty of time to shop for more satisfying food. Just go get a Snickers bar or something.

CLIMBER TAGGED IN PHOTO
Utah, American Fork Canyon, Division Wall

On August 3, two female climbers (both 27 years old) climbed four different routes on the Division Wall after work without incident, but also without inviting a mutual friend of theirs, Denise, who probably would have loved to go climbing. After returning to their car, one of the climbers posted a photo of the other climber to Instagram, and Denise saw the photo, causing hurt feelings and noticeable awkwardness between the three climbing friends.

Analysis: In the age of social media, having good judgment on the appropriateness of sharing a climbing photo is important, especially if Denise is involved, because although she's great otherwise, she's kind of prone to being jealous if we're being completely honest.

TESTICLE CAUGHT IN HARNESS LEG LOOP
Oregon, Smith Rock State Park, Christian Brothers Wall

On March 11, a male climber (26 years old) was climbing Barbecue the Pope and became pumped near the anchors. Unable to hold on, he fell from about six feet above the previous clipped bolt. As the rope caught his fall, his left testicle became painfully pinched between the leg loop of his harness. The climber lowered off the route safely and decided to take the rest of the day off.

Analysis: Proper falling technique is an important skill for all climbers to practice and master, but in this case, a properly-fitting harness or a minor adjustment before leaving the ground may have prevented the ball-smashing.

WRONG COFFEE PACKED
Wyoming, Wind River Range, Cirque of the Towers

On September 5, two climbers (male, 26 years old; female, 26 years old) left their tent to begin preparing for a climb of the Northeast Face when they discovered one of them had accidentally purchased and brought decaffeinated coffee. The climbing trip was aborted.

Analysis: Proper assessment of conditions can be the difference between life or death on a climb, and these climbers showed appropriate prudence in their situation. Although a decaffeinated ascent of one of the Fifty Classic Climbs would have been quite savage.

HARNESS SOILED
Colorado, Rocky Mountain National Park, Lumpy Ridge

On October 4, two climbers (male, 38 years old; male, 36 years old) climbed Pear Buttress on the Left Book formation at Lumpy Ridge. At the top of the formation, the first climber coiled the rope while the second climber stepped away to urinate. While in a rush to empty his bladder, the climber dribbled on the leg loop of his harness before correcting his aiming.

Analysis: The climber is to be commended for not urinating while on a very popular route and waiting until he topped out, even if he did get a little on his harness. At least it was pee and not poop.

ROPE MISCOMMUNICATION
Nevada, Red Rock National Conservation Area, Black Corridor

Two climbers (male, 30 years old, female, 28 years old), arrived at the base of the Black Corridor crag to discover that neither of them had brought a rope, but they each had twelve quickdraws. They retreated from the crag, walked back to their car, drove to the female climber's house, got a rope, and returned to the crag for a slightly shorted day of climbing.

Analysis: When planning for a day of sport climbing, a rope is helpful.

SUNGLASSES ABANDONED
Washington, Stuart Range, Mount Stuart

On August 9, on the descent from the summit of Mount Stuart after a successful climb of the North Ridge route, a male climber (33 years old) discovered he had taken off his sunglasses while sitting on the summit and had forgotten to put them back on before following his partner (female, 34 years old) down, and only discovered his mistake after descending several hundred feet.

Analysis: If anybody's up there in the next couple weeks, they're black Smith sunglasses with polarized lenses.

*These are all fictionalized, but very likely remind you of a climber you know, or a climber you are.

THE CASE FOR GIVING A SHIT

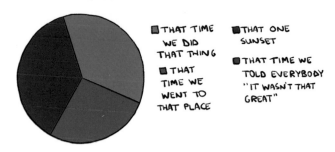

Hilary and I drove four hours to stand on a gravel road north of Scottsbluff, Nebraska, for two minutes of magic on Monday. A couple dozen other cars were parked on the same quarter mile of road, full of people doing the same thing: standing and looking up at the sun, waiting for the moon to move completely in front of it for about ninety nine seconds.

The daylight dimmed around us and the temperature dropped. In the seconds just before totality, shadow bands rippled across the dirt road at our feet. We pulled off our cardboard glasses and stared at it: a black circle with a glowing ring around it. A sort of 360-degree sunset painted the horizon pink all the way around us. From the far end of the road, where most of the cars had parked, cheers erupted.

People were cheering for the solar system. We usually cheer for sports teams, speeches, live performances, but rarely do the sun and the moon get applause. It was a ridiculous and wonderful moment to share with a bunch of strangers, and then it was over. The sun came back out and people jumped in their cars and drove away, to wherever home was.

As Hilary drove, I scrolled through social media, seeing what everyone saw: great photos of the eclipse taken by skilled photographers, photos of families in cardboard sunglasses, friends who had all made pilgrimages to watch the sun and moon do their thing. It was a phenomenon.

And then I discovered on Facebook that even the solar eclipse has haters. People wrote their own takes on it: "Underwhelmed." "That was it?" "Lame." "I should have lowered my expectations." It was like people were going on Yelp to rate a new restaurant in their neighborhood, or reviewing a film that just came out, as if something could be done to meet their personal needs better next time. Universe: Two stars out of five.

Who are we complaining to here? The manager of the solar system? The PR company responsible for all the hype about the eclipse? The company who sold us this rare astronomical event? What would we like for our trouble, a refund?

Not giving a shit is helpful in a lot of circumstances: not caring about non-constructive criticism of your work, not reading hundreds of very similar news articles per day that cause you not only to think the world is ending, but to take over all your productive hours and conversations with friends, focusing on what makes you truly happy instead of working yourself to death just to have a house/car/lawnmower that looks as good as your next-door neighbor's.

But apathy is largely pretty useless and unproductive. Being "too cool" for everything is not establishing your impeccable taste, it's establishing you as a person with a shitty attitude. I don't know about you, but I'll tell you who doesn't get invited back to do fun stuff most of the time: the person who, when everyone else is standing around in the parking lot talking about what a great ride/climb/ski day they had, has to talk about how last Tuesday was better and last time they rode that trail was better and they really don't see what all the hype is about.

Yeah, spending nine hours in the car for two minutes of eclipse was not fun, nor was the traffic. But between the possibility of making a once-in-a-lifetime memory or staying home and pooh-poohing the whole thing, I'll take my chances on the former.

I don't know about you, but I'd rather look back on my life and remember having my mind blown, whether it's experiencing an Arctic sunset, seeing the Grand Canyon for the first or twentieth time, or witnessing a solar eclipse.

The next morning, after seeing the deluge of photos, videos, and other reactions to the eclipse, positive and negative, Hilary said: "I think you can choose to have wonder in your life, or not."

THE COFFEE DRINKER'S GUIDE TO BEING PRESENT

About five years ago, my friend Tommy told me what I thought was an insignificant thing: that he'd taken a ceramic mug to his office and had started using that for his morning coffee instead of a travel mug. He said it made him feel less rushed.

In the span of those five years, Tommy's little seed of an idea stuck with me, and gradually and almost subconsciously grew into a full-blown life philosophy. I too tried to start drinking out of ceramic mugs when possible. I minimized drinking coffee in a car, preferring to schedule a few minutes for drinking coffee somewhere stationary, whether it was my apartment or a coffee shop. Every coffee shop I visited, I specified "for here" to avoid being served coffee in a paper cup. I noticed at hotels and sometimes airport coffee shops in Europe, coffee was served in ceramic mugs, and how much I liked it compared to a hotel breakfast in the U.S., served on all disposable dishes and cups. (Obviously it's also better for the planet if we're not creating a piece of trash every time we drink a cup of coffee, but I'm talking about something else here.)

I wouldn't have expected that concept to change my life in a big way, but now I look at to-go cups and travel mugs like the equivalent of drinking wine out of a glass vs. straight out of the bottle. Or maybe more accurately, sitting down to eat a sandwich at an actual table vs. wolfing down a drive-through meal while navigating in freeway traffic. I've learned to like my coffee like I like my conversations with good friends: not rushed.

But we all feel rushed, don't we? We live in a world that seems to get faster and faster every month. And how do we deal with it? Most of us try to adapt and keep up with it all, without even thinking about it. We have eight different methods people can use to contact us and we have to check them every fifteen minutes just in case we missed something. We eat lunch at our desks, and drink our coffee out of non-spill vessels, often in our cars. And nobody just sits and drinks coffee anymore, except one legendary Starbucks customer spotted in 2015.

Yes, it's great that we've been able to make lots of things portable, including drinking coffee. But while the actual coffee is portable, the experience of slowing down and taking a minute to be present is not so much.

Maybe my friend Tommy is onto something with his ceramic coffee mug, and he knows something most of us should admit: that rushing the things we love isn't making us any happier—even if it is making us able to scroll through 12 to 15 more meters of social media feeds every day. Maybe instead of trying so hard to keep up with everything, we should all take a small step in resisting the velocity of our discontent.

THE SHORTCUT IS:
THERE IS NO SHORTCUT

Here's something that didn't happen. Tommy Caldwell, in the days following the first ascent of the Dawn Wall, being interviewed by a journalist about how he did it, said: "Well, I'm sure it looks like a lot of work to climb this thing, but I have this one trick move that I do and it's really easy for me."

Also something that didn't happen. Lael Wilcox, just after becoming the first American to win the Trans Am Bike Race, tweeted: "I don't really train at all. I just eat Brand X energy bars and they make me really fast."

You can probably imagine similar stories *not* coming from successful authors, entrepreneurs, and athletes. We love the story of a hardworking person putting in the hours, the blood, sweat, and tears to realize their dreams. Or do we?

A few years ago, I was talking to a person who wanted to become a writer, and that person said to me, "I'm sick of people telling me I need to put in my dues to get to where I want to go. At this point, I want a shortcut." And every few weeks, I get a message from an aspiring creative asking for some tips, tricks, or secrets on how to get started as a writer or filmmaker. I don't have tips, tricks, or secrets on how to make it easy for anyone, and I'd guess no one else does either. I suggest a two-step process that seems to work for people if you also apply something called "patience":

- Step 1: Make the best thing you can every time, as often as you can do it.
- Step 2: Stick with it for a few years.

If you get to the top of your climbing project the first time you try to lead it, guess what? It's not a project. You'll lower off, thinking, "Holy shit, that was much easier than I expected," and you'll move on to something that's a real challenge. Because that's what you want: something that will push you mentally and physically and help you grow. That's the point—not walking into a climbing gym for the first time, cruising up everything, congratulating yourself on your immense natural talent, and moving on to the next hobby. That's why people climb for years before they think they're anywhere close to "good at it"—or write for years before they feel like they've found their voice, or paint for years, or whatever.

In the era of clickbait articles and listicles, we love "hacks," tips, tricks, and shortcuts. You can hack some things: opening jars, technology, occasionally your burrito order. But nothing long-term worth working for can be hacked, and if it can be hacked, it won't be nearly as meaningful.

Sure, we love shows like *American Idol*, because they perpetuate a one-in-a-million dream-coming-true story. But none of the people on that show got on that stage without trying hard for a long time before the moment we see them on TV. They weren't standing in line at Starbucks and then said, "Oh hey, look, they're having auditions across the street, I used to sing a little bit in middle school, maybe I'll get in line and see if I can remember all the lines to 'Waiting on a Friend,' and then all of a sudden impress the judges enough to get on the show." That's not how anything works.

Not even performance-enhancing drugs are a shortcut. I mean, look at every single cyclist ever caught doping: Do they look like they spent the past few years sitting on the couch eating Funyuns and playing Call of Duty, but knew a guy who knew a guy who could get them the proper pharmaceuticals to get them on a podium at a cycling race? Fuck no, they trained their asses off, AND they took illegal drugs.

You want a shortcut, here's one: Stop believing that anyone who's successful at anything has some secret other than focus, drive, and a shitload of hard work. There's your shortcut.

WHAT WAS THAT NOISE OUTSIDE THE TENT?

Did you hear that? What was that noise outside the tent? Some possibilities:

A BEAR

That noise was a bear. That bear is going to either interact with you in a violent manner, or leave you alone. Did you accidentally bring a Snickers bar inside the tent? Well, that's proving to be a huge mistake, isn't it? You're going to die.

AN ANIMAL MUCH SMALLER THAN A BEAR

That noise was a squirrel, or a mouse, or a pika, or some other animal so small it can't kill you. You will likely not die tonight, but you will eventually, of course, die. We all do.

FLATULENCE

That noise was a fart. It was not outside the tent, it was inside the tent, coming from your tentmate. No matter how bad it smells, you will most likely not die from the smell. In the morning, you can talk to your tentmate about it, and you may exaggerate the potency of the smell for comic effect, i.e., "Jesus H. Christ, Kevin, you farted in your sleep last night. What did you eat? I thought I was going to die."

A DIPSHIT

That noise was that dipshit Terry, who got hammered and passed out in a camp chair next to the fire after an evening of loud pointless stories, interrupting and annoying the shit out of everyone, and no one felt like waking him up before they all put out the campfire and turned in for the night. Terry has tipped over his camp chair and fallen to the ground. No one knows who invited Terry. You could get up and see if he's OK, or you could recall that he vaguely insulted your career earlier, and then roll over in your sleeping bag and go back to sleep. I mean, he's not going to die out there. Plus he's an adult. An adult douchebag.

THE PROVERBIAL TREE FALLING IN THE FOREST

That noise was a tree falling in the forest, which would have made a sound whether you were here to hear it or not. Humans are not the only animals with a sense of hearing. You are probably not going to die unless the sound of it falling was really close to your tent, in which case you don't have a hell of a lot of time to think about it, and certainly not enough time to unzip your sleeping bag, unzip the tent door, and run. So yeah, if that noise was a tree falling on your tent, you might die.

YOUR ANXIETIES, WHICH ARE BEST TO THINK ABOUT BETWEEN THE HOURS OF 1 A.M. AND 4 A.M.

That noise was a gentle reminder from the universe to you, reminding you to worry about some stuff: Are you sure you locked your car at the trailhead? Did you definitely lock the door of your apartment? Shut the garage door? Did you pay your mortgage this month? Is your car overdue for an oil change? Are you really fulfilled in your job? Have you taken enough Instagram-worthy photos on this trip? Do you even like camping? None of these answers are going to cause you to die (at least not immediately), but if you don't calm down and get back to sleep, you might feel like you're dying from lack of rest tomorrow.

THE GEARS OF THE MACHINATIONS OF INTERNET COMMUNICATION

That noise was an email making its way across the internet and into your inbox, which, statistically speaking, is something likely to happen several times during your camping trip. Was it from your boss? A client? Was it one of the thrice-daily emails you receive from a hotel loyalty program? There's no way of knowing, all the way out here in your tent in the middle of nowhere, far from cell service. Isn't this horrible? Email is not going to kill you, but constantly worrying about it is probably kind of ruining your life, if you think about it.

JASON VOORHEES

That noise was Jason Voorhees, a killer who wears a hockey mask and stalks his victims before killing them in a gruesome and sometimes rather creative manner. You will die in the next sixty to ninety minutes.

THE WIND

That noise was just the wind or something, relax. Unless "something" means "Jason Voorhees" or "a bear," because then you're fucked.

HAPPINESS IS YOUR BACKYARD TRAIL

I plodded my way up the Hayden Trail, heading up toward my fifth "summit" of the day as the sun coasted downward. I had eaten my last Clif Shot a while ago, and had drunk my last water with it. Most of the mountain bikers and hikers had gone home for the day, and I was clocking my fifth hour running around Green Mountain, attempting a contrived trail run in which I ran down every trail leading from the summit and then back up. I had miscalculated the distance, elevation gain, and food and water needed (by not trying to calculate it at all and just guessing). I was having a bit of an adventure, a little over 11 miles from my house, which I could theoretically see from the top of Green Mountain.

Green Mountain is nothing special by Colorado standards: a 6,854-foot mesa at the edge of the Denver suburbs, rising about 800 feet above the roads that border it, two of which are freeways. Calling it a mountain is a bit comical when you look at the range of peaks that rise literally right behind it (on a clear day, you can see three 14,000-foot peaks from the summit). It's not even the most famous "Green Mountain" in the Front Range—Boulder's Green Mountain holds the famous Flatirons on its east face, and Chautauqua Park below those.

The Green Mountain I run on is a big hill, lacking the forested trails and rocky crags of its taller, steeper neighbors.

But I love that goddamn big hill with no trees, sitting in front of the "real" mountains. It has 17.5 miles of trails, and I've run, walked, and mountain biked at least a thousand miles on those trails. None of them lead to a breathtaking waterfall or across a creek or a river. People don't even take selfies on the summit—it's kind of just a flat area that sometimes has a cairn on it. But like an old loyal dog or a reliable but scratched-up old bicycle, it's mine. Or rather, it's ours—myself and the dozens of people whose cars fill the Green Mountain parking lots on weekends and after work on weekdays.

For every Instagram-worthy, magazine-cover-headline-inspiring, do-this-before-you-die trail, there are thousands of miles of unsung (or lesser-sung) trails like those. When people ask, "What's your favorite trail?" we tell them some trail we've been on once or twice in our lives, instead of the one we could walk blindfolded. And we keep going back to our backyard trails not because of one or two unforgettable experiences, but because of dozens of good experiences.

Green Mountain's trails are usually the first ones to dry out in the spring or after a snowstorm, and plenty of people know it. I'm used to sharing it with a few dozen hikers, runners, bikers, and dogs on weekends, but also watching hundreds of cars drive past it to head up I-70 to go skiing for the day. Lots of days it's what you might call "crowded," but some days you get the place to yourself for a few minutes—near sunrise, when you might surprise a rattlesnake or two, or near sunset, when you might hear the haunting, party howls of a pack of coyotes somewhere nearby.

Hell, you know what, my favorite trail is not Angel's Landing in Zion National Park, or the Glacier Gorge Trail in Rocky Mountain National Park, or the Hardergrat in Switzerland. It's a few miles of trails in William Frederick Hayden Park on Green Mountain twenty-five minutes from my house, which I talk about like someone talks about an old car and all its quirks: there's no shade in the summer, it doesn't get very high, the trails aren't technical at all, sometimes on a busy Saturday you have to step off the trail thirty or forty times to let people pass, it gets windy on the top, there are snakes in the summertime, I've been up there so many times it kind of feels like going to the gym, there's nowhere to hide if you have to unexpectedly use the bathroom

. . . but still, it's my favorite. You know, this old thing? It's no John Muir Trail, but I guess it's pretty OK.

Last Sunday, as the sun started to dip below the mountains to the west, I jogged off the top of Green Mountain to head down to my car to finally get some food and water. I saw five people total in the last mile of fire road to the parking lot, downright peaceful for a busy Sunday. Peaceful enough that a deer stood in the middle of the fire road, looking up at me until I got about 80 feet from it and it bounded into the next gully—where twenty of its friends waited, all staring at me in the last minutes of golden sunlight. OK, yeah, this is my favorite trail.

TWENTY-FIVE THINGS SAID THAT MIGHT MEAN YOU'RE GOING TO HAVE AN EPIC

In this context, "epic" means a very long day, not like a "we're-gonna die" epic.

1. "You'll be fine."
2. "I'm pretty sure it's this way."
3. "We don't need a map."
4. "I know where I'm going."
5. "Seems to be a bit further than I thought."
6. "There's a bit of bushwhacking."
7. "The guidebook said to go up the 'obvious gully.'"
8. "We don't need raingear—it's not supposed to rain until later."
9. "Hope you're OK with a little breakable crust."
10. "I have an excellent natural sense of direction."
11. "I don't remember it being this overgrown."
12. "Hopefully it's just this short section of postholing."
13. "For some reason, I thought it didn't get dark until later."

14. "No, I'm pretty sure I heard you say back at the car that you packed the tent poles."
15. "Those are not storm clouds. Those are just big, tall, puffy clouds."
16. "That's what I forgot to buy—batteries for this headlamp."
17. "I'm 90 percent sure we go left here."
18. "So I looked through my whole pack, and it turns out I only brought one climbing shoe."
19. "Wow, these dehydrated meals have a lot of fiber in them. Like a lot a lot."
20. "It says to look for 'a faint climbers' trail.'"
21. "Wow, I guess it really is true that when you're lost, you walk in circles."
22. "I dropped the rack."
23. "The good news is, we will still have 15 meters of rope left."
24. "How many times do I have to tell you, we're not lost."
25. "I thought it was just going to be a fart."

COMPLAINING IS USELESS

OUTDOOR ADVENTURE COMPLAINT CHART

IT'S SNOWING ➡ AT LEAST IT'S NOT RAINING

IT'S RAINING ➡ AT LEAST IT'S NOT COLD + WINDY

IT'S COLD + WINDY ➡ AT LEAST IT'S NOT RAINING TOO

IT'S COLD, WINDY, RAINING, + SNOWING ➡ AT LEAST WE'RE NOT AT WORK

One Sunday last August, maybe halfway through a 22-mile trail run in 85 degrees and full sun, the day after we'd run 24 trail miles as part of a training schedule, I said to my friend Jayson something along the lines of, "It's definitely warm today."

Jayson, sarcastically and appropriately, replied: "Thanks, I hadn't thought about that."

I historically have tended toward negative thinking, but for about the past 15 years, have gravitated toward people like Jayson who do not. And because of that, I have learned the utter uselessness of complaining about things I can't change—like the fact that during the summer, it's often hot outside. In the winter, it's often cold outside. Sometimes when we want to do things outdoors, it's windy. Or it's rainy. Or the things we like to do make our feet hurt, or our shoulders. Or we have to carry heavy backpacks to get somewhere to do something. And whining about it does exactly nothing to help.

I climbed a lot with my friend Lee for about six years, and the general theme we arrived at through many long hours in uncomfortable positions was that pretty much every problem you have in the mountains is your own fault, and there's no sense in complaining about it. Cold? Should have brought more layers. Tired? Should have gone to bed earlier before our 3 a.m. start. Getting rained on? Could have waited for a day with a better weather forecast. Scared of a hard move on a climb? Should have trained more and gotten stronger. Handhold or foothold broke? That's geology; rocks don't last forever.

Usually one of us would acknowledge the ridiculousness of our uncomfortable hobby with the same joke, which neither of us ever laughed at: "You know, we could be at home watching golf on TV right now."

My grandmother used to be fond of the saying, "You can wish in one hand and shit in the other one and see which one fills up first," which is a way of saying that if you're not going to do anything to fix a problem, talking about it just to talk about it is pointless. Whoever originated that saying was, however many decades back, talking about what Dr. Travis Bradberry calls "solution-oriented complaining." Bradberry says you should minimize complaining, because of its negative effects on many areas of your mental and physical health, but if you do complain, make sure it has a purpose other than just venting.

I've learned to rein in my negative thoughts over the years, realizing the friends I hang out with don't really want to hear them, and it's helped me to minimize them or eliminate them in my own head. If it's hot, acknowledge it and review things I need to be doing to deal with it: hydrate, slow down, find a pace that won't result in heatstroke. If it's cold, I make sure my clothing is layered so I'm not sweating and my extremities aren't going numb. If it's windy, I just laugh and try to stay upright.

I've also listened to a lot of interviews with people who succeed—whether in climbing mountains or other pursuits—and I started to notice a trend: None of them seem to complain their way to the top—they are good at finding solutions, not whining about problems. We'd probably all do better to follow their lead, even when it's hot outside, or cold, or windy, or raining, or snowing.

I MUST HAVE MY COFFEE FIRST THING IN THE MORNING

MORNING: A TIMELINE

SLEEP — DON'T EVEN FUCKING TALK TO ME — COFFEE — LUNCH

If I don't have coffee immediately upon waking up, I cannot function in any capacity that a human being is supposed to function. I cannot work, I cannot communicate with other sentient beings, I cannot be friendly or even reasonable. I am essentially a houseplant until I have had this magical bitter bean water stimulant to which I have been addicted for the majority of my adult life. I am a houseplant, but also a tiger.

Before I have performed my daily sacred coffee-drinking ritual, I certainly cannot be expected to not maim or kill other people or animals in fits of unprovoked murderous rage. Give me coffee, or face severe consequences.

You of course know what I'm talking about. Perhaps you have at one time or another shared a meme that contained the phrase "but first, coffee," or you own a T-shirt with that phrase on it, gifted to you by a friend or relative who understands or at least tolerates your intolerance for all other life-forms in the minutes before you have consumed water filtered through ground coffee beans. Perhaps you, like me, have that phrase tattooed on your neck in block letters.

I will have coffee immediately upon exiting my sleeping quarters, before I perform any other tasks that require even the feeblest amount of brain activity. I will not brush my teeth, I will not turn on lights, I will not urinate. How could it be demanded of me that I manage to do something as involved as peeing before I've had coffee? This is 2018. If my entire day were made into a to-do list, "coffee" would be No. 1 on that list, followed by everything else that, let's be honest, is not going to fucking happen unless I drink coffee first.

If my house caught fire in the middle of the night and my spouse were to wake me up and demand that we flee the building immediately lest we perish in flames, I would tell my spouse I'm not going anywhere until I've had a decent cup of coffee. I would stand there as tongues of fire licked the walls around me and the kitchen filled with smoke and I would brew my coffee with my eyes mostly closed, and when it was finished I would pour it into a cup, take a sip, and then shuffle out of the house.

Perhaps you have seen action movies in which a character violently destroys another human being, a group of human beings, an entire civilization, an entire planet, for one reason or another. No matter what the reason, when I watch movies and there is an incredible amount of death and destruction being doled out by a character, I always nod in understanding, and in my head I say, "That's me before I've had coffee."

It's true. Liam Neeson in *Taken*, kicking the shit out of everyone who gets in his way as he tries to get his kidnapped daughter back? Me, except replace "kidnapped daughter" with "coffee." Charlize Theron annihilating everyone who messes with her in *Atomic Blonde*? Me, just because I haven't had coffee yet and something is in my way. The Starkiller Base superweapon destroying five planets in *Star Wars: The Force Awakens*? You get the picture. Good guys, bad guys, it doesn't matter. I relate, because when it comes to coffee, anything that gets in my way is a bad guy, and I will resort to any means necessary to get that coffee.

I'm not a monster, or a bad person. I very simply need my coffee, immediately. So please understand this and stay out of my way, or prepare to die. Thanks.

THE GAS TANK IS ONE-QUARTER FULL, OR THREE-QUARTERS EMPTY

"WE'LL BE FINE"

"WE'RE ALMOST OUT OF GAS"

Just east of Green River, Utah, on Interstate 70, I looked over from the passenger seat to see the car's gas gauge hovering around a quarter full. I mentally catalogued the distance and number of gas stations between us and the Hot Tomato in Fruita, Colorado, and could only remember one in those 90 miles.

"Maybe we should stop and get some gas," I said to my friend Forest.

"I think we're good, don't you?" Forest replied.

Forest is a photographer, and we've known each other for almost six years. We've spent dozens of days together, collaborating on outdoor magazine articles, adventure films, and now a book project—and we approach things from almost complete opposite ideologies. You might say I'm a bit more of a planner, and he flies by the seat of his pants. I like to say that the world takes care of Forest, but I don't trust the world to take care of me. I eliminate as many variables as possible prior to doing something—he more or less lets the variables fall where they may.

And there we were last Thursday, in eastern Utah, both looking at the gas gauge but seeing completely different things. We discussed the gas tank capacity of my car (16.9 gallons), the average miles per gallon the car got on the highway (up to 27 miles per gallon), and how far we had to go to the next known gas station (about 80 miles). Mathematically, we were right on that line between We'll Be Fine vs. We're Going to Run Out of Gas. Which is a classic "There are two types of people in this world" debate.

I asked Forest, "Have you ever run out of gas?"

He laughed. "Several times."

"I never have," I said.

"One of those times I ran out of gas," Forest said, "I got out of the car and there was a gas can sitting off to the side of the road, and I had pulled over just down the hill from a gas station. So I grabbed the gas can, jogged up to the gas station, filled it up, and the whole thing only cost me about fifteen minutes."

"That is the most Forest Woodward story of all time," I said.

"I was on my way to the airport, too." Of course he was.

We started talking about the differences in the ways we view the world. I book flights weeks in advance. Forest books flights a couple days in advance. I have 11 unread emails in my inbox right now, and he has more than 2,500 unread emails in his inbox. I can go years without losing a water bottle or travel mug, and, well, Forest can go weeks, or days. Two days prior to our drive through Utah, we had run 37 miles across Zion National Park, and Forest had worn trail running shoes with almost no tread on them, with three-inch rips in each instep, and with laces barely hanging onto enough of the shoe to stay on his feet. And his water bottles were leaking.

Despite, or maybe because of, this difference in thinking, this massive chasm between our ideas of How To Do Things, we enjoy each other's company and (in my opinion) work well together on creative projects. Ten years ago, even being in close proximity to his laissez-faire planning would have driven me nuts, but nowadays I try to watch him, remind myself to relax, and not try to control everything. Because it always seems to work out for Forest. Of course, he notes an asterisk to that statement, that even though it always works out, it can sometimes be expensive, and he has definitely missed a few emails that might have meant the successful sale of a photo or two.

But, it always works out for me, too—no matter how much I try to control things, or just let them go—even if the way it works out isn't how I imagined it. Flights get delayed, it rains when I don't want it to, bikes get flat tires, avalanche conditions are terrible sometimes, packages get lost in shipping, and in the end, our story isn't something any of us are in control of, whether we think we are or not. The one thing Forest and I agree on is that whether you plan or don't plan, you can't get angry and try to place blame on someone else when things don't work out. Because whether you believe you can control things or you don't worry at all about trying to control things, shit happens. And when it does, nobody wants to be that jerk with a vein popping out of their forehead as they scream at an airline employee about how important they are.

Last year, I read an essay titled "Do You Want to Be Known for Your Writing, or for Your Swift Email Responses?" and I realized, shit, I actually would love to focus on my creative work more than I focus on answering email promptly. I'm trying, but it's a battle to even pretend to ignore my inbox. Or gas gauge.

We pulled off at exit 15 for Loma, Colorado, and both sighed, Forest more than me, as I announced that we still had 1.3 miles, mostly downhill, to the Conoco station north of I-70. We made it, filled the car up with gas, and were not late for the film festival we were driving to that evening. It worked out. The world continues to take care of Forest, I continue to not totally trust the world to take care of me. But when we're in the same car with a quarter-tank of gas, as a friend once told me, "One way or another, it'll work itself out."

ACKNOWLEDGMENTS

This book would not exist if it were not for Hilary Oliver, my wife, creative partner, and primary editor of anything that makes it out of my brain and onto the internet. Her eye, intellect, and sensitivity have prevented countless disasters, missteps, and written and drawn pieces of questionable taste since 2012.

Steve Casimiro, outdoor media legend and guru, was the first person to believe the stories on Semi-Rad.com were worthy of a larger audience. Since 2011, Steve has been an editor, inspiration, and dear friend. I shudder to think about what my career would look like if Steve had never noticed my stuff.

Christian Folk and several other friends at Outdoor Research have supported Semi-Rad.com and my adventures since 2011, through several periods of time when the blog might have ceased to exist if not for OR's support keeping the creative lights on, so to speak.

Ian Anderson at Backbone Media, way back in 2012, was the first person to encourage me to pursue outdoor industry sponsorship and then connect me to people who made that possible—for what was then a very fledgling outdoor media website.

Out of all the people who read and share my stories and art, I am most thankful for the few hundred people who support my work financially via Patreon. At the end of the day, I make things because of that inner circle, who come from all over the United States and the world.

I've had a few dozen wonderful friends who have invited me on adventures, joined me on adventures, and inspired some adventures, and have either become subjects of stories on Semi-Rad.com, or seen our conversations end up in stories on Semi-Rad.com. Thanks to all of you who have given me a belay, shared a tent, broken trail, sat across a campfire, or hung on during one of those days that seemed like it was never going to end—I am sure you all know who you are.

My old friend Josh Barker gave me a couple pieces of great advice before I started Semi-Rad.com, and in its first couple years that advice became a big part of the blog's foundation.

And finally, thanks to Kate, Laura, Emily, Darryl, Helen, and the staff at Mountaineers Books who made this book a reality.

ABOUT THE AUTHOR

Brendan Leonard is the creator of Semi-Rad.com, an author, and filmmaker. He has directed and codirected several award-winning adventure films, including *How to Run 100 Miles*, *Chocolate Spokes*, *Ace and the Desert Dog*, and *Frank and the Tower*. He's a columnist for *Outside* magazine and a contributing editor at *Adventure Journal*, and his writing has appeared on CNN.com and in *Runner's World*, *Climbing*, *Alpinist*, *Men's Journal*, *Backpacker*, *Adventure Cyclist*, and dozens of other publications. His other books include *Sixty Meters to Anywhere* and *The Great Outdoors: A User's Guide*.

YOU MAY ALSO LIKE: